D0857506

FULFILLING
THE PROMISE OF
CHILDREN'S
SERVICES

David G. Blumenkrantz

Foreword by
Seymour B. Sarason

FULFILLING THE PROMISE OF CHILDREN'S SERVICES

Why Primary Prevention Efforts Fail and How They Can Succeed

Jossey-Bass Publishers · San Francisco

Copyright © 1992 by Jossey-Bass Inc., Publishers, 350 Sansome Street, San Francisco, California 94104. Copyright under International, Pan American, and Universal Copyright Conventions. All rights reserved. No part of this book may be reproduced in any form—except for brief quotation (not to exceed 1,000 words) in a review or professional work—without permission in writing from the publishers.

For sales outside the United States, contact Maxwell Macmillan International Publishing Group, 866 Third Avenue, New York, New York 10022.

Manufactured in the United States of America.

The paper used in this book is acid-free and meets the State of California requirements for recycled paper (50 percent recycled waste, including 10 percent postconsumer waste), which are the strictest guidelines for recycled paper currently in use in the United States.

Library of Congress Cataloging-in-Publication Data

Blumenkrantz, David G., date.
   Fulfilling the promise of children's services : why primary prevention efforts fail and how they can succeed / David G. Blumenkrantz.
      p.   cm.—(The Jossey-Bass social and behavioral science series)
   Includes bibliographical references and index.
   ISBN 1-55542-450-3
   1. Children—Services for—United States. 2. Social work with children—United States. I. Title. II. Series.
HV741.B58   1992
362.7′1′0973—dc20   92-73
                                               CIP

Rite of Passage Experience© and ROPE® are copyrighted and registered marks of David G. Blumenkrantz.

Permission to quote from the "Report on the Evaluation of the ROPE Program, Cohorts 1–5," by Jacquelyn A. Hawkins, was granted by the Town of East Hartford's Department of Youth Services.

FIRST EDITION
HB Printing   10 9 8 7 6 5 4 3 2 1   *Code 9253*

362.71
B65

93.1401
25164933

*The Jossey-Bass
Social and Behavioral Science Series*

Contents

Part Three: Primary Prevention Training in Communities

Part Four: Practical Lessons and Future Directions

Foreword

The post-World War II era has witnessed a truly extraordinary increase in the number and diversity of human service agencies in the public and voluntary sectors. Accompanying this increase has been a growing literature on the nature and effectiveness of these agencies. The bulk of this literature must be characterized as spotty in terms of quality, comprehensiveness, and even relevance. It would not be unfair to describe it as largely anecdotal, leaving readers uncertain about how well goals have been achieved. Few descriptions or evaluations provide a rosy picture. Indeed, it is hard to escape the impression that, generally speaking, these new agencies, despite the best of intentions and heroic efforts, are far from meeting their intended purposes. Why this is so is usually unclear. Is it underfunding? inadequately selected and trained personnel? turfdom and bureaucratic entanglements? politics (local, state, and national)? misguided initial conceptualizations of the problems to be attacked? From the standpoint of these questions, the existing literature is not at all helpful. We do not know what we have or should have learned. It is also the case that this literature has had virtually no impact on policies, on legislation, or even on the continued existence of these human services agencies.

I have had countless opportunities to observe and consult with these agencies, and I have come away with several firm conclusions. The first conclusion is that, more often than not, the staff of such agencies are young, hardworking, idealistic people. What they may lack in background or formal training is partially compensated for by motivation and creative maneuvering. The second conclusion is that these young people know that the policy rhetoric that justified the creation of the new agencies has slowly (and sometimes rapidly) transformed the agencies in ways antithetical to that rhetoric, with the result that staff morale has been weakened. The third conclusion is related to the second: the staff of these agencies understand that the implications of that policy rhetoric were never really thought through; since it was a rhetoric of virtue whose practical consequences were never systematically understood and confronted, when the rhetoric came face-to-face with social, political, and institutional realities, its emptiness became obvious. A fourth conclusion, one most relevant to the present volume, is that the leaders and staff of these agencies are very sophisticated about why the agencies are so deficient in meeting goals and being effective but are unable, unwilling, or too constrained to write about what they know and have experienced. They represent a kind of clinician-activist, not schooled to write up their experience for what it can tell us about the relationship between goals and practice in the real world, and yet what they can tell us is of vital theoretical and practical importance.

These conclusions explain my enthusiasm when I learned that David G. Blumenkrantz, long a warrior in the human services arena, had begun to outline a book on a new species of human service agency: the Youth Service Bureau, of which hundreds have been created in recent decades in communities around the country. Blumenkrantz, as a longtime director of such an agency in a city of modest size, was in a position to examine these bureaus in his own community and in others in his state and around the country. What is so refreshing is his awareness that the problems he confronted are common to these new community agencies. He has sought to understand why and how these agencies are not meeting their intended purposes. For example, they were created to devise and implement preventive programs, not to come up with "quick fixes" for problems that are already overwhelming and difficult, if not insoluble. They were intended as catalysts for proactive community efforts, as vehicles for involving the community and helping it use its resources to prevent problems. But things did not work out that way, and David Blumenkrantz tells us why.

He does more than that, however. Several chapters of this book describe the Rite of Passage Experience (ROPE), a program explicitly preventive in orientation and requiring the participation of parents, schoolchildren, and school personnel. Blumenkrantz does not describe ROPE as a panacea; indeed, he tells about the obstacles that the program's implementation encounters in diverse communities and about the conditions that must exist if the program is to have the desired effects. ROPE is an example of what could and should be done to give a Youth Service Bureau a truly community-oriented, preventive character.

One of the distinctive features of this book is that it is written in the first person, which allows us more than a glimpse of a bureau chief struggling with pressures, crises, and community politics as he tries to be true to his vision and values and see beyond today in a particular community while exposing his own frailties, anxieties, and passions. If we had more such accounts from people on the firing line in our human services agencies, we would stand a better chance of making practice more consistent with policy rhetoric. Academics have written much about policy and values, and many have written up their evaluations of these agencies. But precisely because they are not on the firing line, they cannot know or use the phenomenological substance and context of those whose lives center on practice, and without that substance and context, their evaluations ignore crucial data that should inform change.

This is far more than a book about Youth Service Bureaus. It is a book relevant to the policy arena, to community resources and involvement, to issues of primary and secondary prevention, to public schools, and to the ubiquitous problem of individual behavior in bureaucratic settings.

June 1992   Seymour B. Sarason
Professor of Psychology Emeritus
Yale University

*For David and Harris Blumenkrantz—
The past and the future*

Preface

This book is for anyone who has ever asked, "If we can put a man on the moon, create a baby in a test tube, build bridges across great expanses, and erect buildings way up into the sky, then why, with all this technology, can't we help more of our children become responsible, healthy, productive adults?" For almost two decades, I have been attempting to answer this question by developing reasonable program strategies. Creating and implementing strategies that help communities develop healthy, caring, capable young people continues to be an elusive and systematically unachievable task.

Fulfilling the Promise of Children's Services is about the reality of implementing primary prevention strategies. It is unlike many other books on primary prevention in that it does not offer a traditional academic treatment of the subject. Rather, it employs a series of stories to illustrate key concepts essential for the successful delivery of community-based primary prevention initiatives.

During the last ten years, I have been a human services administrator in a community-based public agency. I have served on the boards of directors of many not-for-profit human service agencies, as well as on state government committees and commissions, state senate select subcommittees, and the like. I have been integrally involved, over a long period, with a community and a state struggling to make a better place for children. Simultaneously, I have been an itinerant consultant and trainer, catching brief glimpses of similarly struggling communities across the country. I also created a model for primary preventive community intervention, the Rite of Passage Experience (ROPE*), which I have been pleased to help communities implement across the country. The combination of my experiences has given me a unique professional vantage point.

Although this book is grounded in the theoretical underpinnings of prevention and organizational and community psychology, I wrote it for a broader audience. My goal was to take the potentially dry subjects of prevention and human services and make them come alive in such a way as to compel the reader to ask, "Why do our children's problems keep getting worse? Why can't the human services business do something about it?"

This book offers a unique picture of the culture of public human services agencies. It does not attempt to provide extensive descriptions of a variety of prevention strategies, but it does use a specific prevention strategy to illustrate the practical problems of delivering primary prevention services, and it details the reasons why primary prevention has been largely ineffective.

In part, *Fulfilling the Promise of Children's Services* offers a bridge between two critical elements that affect the delivery of human services: practice and emotion. Consider the national debate over the "drug and alcohol crisis." Emotionally charged catch phrases like "war on drugs" and "just say no" bring attention to the issue but do little else of any benefit. By and large, such slogans and other "quick fix" approaches interfere with uses of prevention technology that are supported by theory, especially in the development and delivery of services.

This book describes the challenges and complexities of planning and delivering primary prevention services to communities. The services that I describe and to which I refer are systematically employed by communities to help their children develop in a positive and healthy way and avoid the onset of problems. We cannot expect primary prevention initiatives to be successful if we fail to understand the conditions that must exist for their success. In the absence of such clearly identifiable conditions, predictable problems will always occur. This book outlines and describes the minimum conditions necessary for the successful development, implementation, and growth of a comprehensive primary prevention strategy that can help a community help its children grow up in our complex world.

Audience

Fulfilling the Promise of Children's Services is intended for people concerned with and interested in programs and agencies for youth and families. Those in the fields of community psychology and public education will find it informative, as will community leaders or citizens interested in helping children. The book will appeal to everyone who has an interest in how the human service system attempts to fulfill the promise of providing prevention services to children. Its narrative vignettes vividly portray the complex relationships between people and institutions that challenge our capacity to really help our children.

Overview of the Contents

Part One describes the foundation on which the delivery of human services occurs. It shows how services struggle to exist in the first place, and then how they attempt to help others. Chapter One gives a bird's-eye view of a day in a community-based agency, where limited resources are strained by the tremendous demand for services responding to crises and problems. Someone may actually be trying to plan and deliver primary prevention services thoughtfully but ends up serving as a "war correspondent" on the front lines, responding to the incoming artillery of social and economic change. This is a day, like many other days in human services, spent in damage control.

Chapter Two describes the context in which community-based human services are provided and examines the origins of the Youth Service Bureau system, whose purpose is to foster collaboration and coordination of resources within communities. Here, we begin to uncover a central element that undermines the effective delivery of human services, especially primary prevention. The limitations of leadership and the impact of legislation are described as they concern the ineffective delivery of primary prevention services.

Chapter Three begins to examine the benefits of primary prevention and the challenges of developing and implementing community intervention strategies. Here, we explore the concept of prevention and how it has been misunderstood and underutilized.

Part Two provides an extensive description of the Rite of Passage Experience (ROPE). ROPE is based on the rite of passage ceremonies of our early ancestors, who practiced "primal prevention" in their efforts to help children make a positive transition to adulthood. Chapter Four introduces a *process* approach to responding to "problems of living," rather than a "quick fix" *program*. The examples in Chapters Five through Eight highlight the complexity of a three-phase, six-year comprehensive primary prevention strategy, illustrating the minimum conditions for the development, implementation, and maintenance of a community intervention for primary prevention.

Chapter Five describes a powerful introduction for parents, students, and community participants to the Rite of Passage Experience. It demonstrates how a prevention program can empower parents and the community to support youth on their journey through adolescence.

Chapter Six continues to illustrate the Rite of Passage Experience program through a detailed description of the first student session. The teaching method as well as the technology of experiential education is described and explained.

Chapter Seven presents an example of a "culminating challenge" offered to students at the end of the first phase of the Rite of Passage Experience. It rejoins the group described in Chapter Six as they attempt to rock climb and rappel.

Chapter Eight briefly describes the second and third phase of the community Rite of Passage Experience. These phases occur for youth in the middle/junior high school and high school. They highlight the process that links youth to positive leisure-time activities in the second phase. The third phase focuses on connecting youth to community service.

Chapter Nine identifies and describes ten elements essential to implementing a primary prevention strategy. It examines how each of these ten elements represents a key ingredient essential for successfully implementing community interventions. It presents an illustration of how challenging it is to initiate a community program.

Chapter Ten presents a number of important guiding principles to consider during the formation of community partnerships. It sets out points of reference for the case studies in subsequent chapters as well as exploring whether prevention is an art or science.

Part Three (Chapters Eleven through Fourteen) describes what happened when different communities around the country attempted to implement the primary prevention strategy described in Part Two. The descriptions reflect the minimum necessary conditions and highlight the importance of developing a process for implementing and sustaining these complex, comprehensive projects. Chapter Eleven describes how a prevention program is successfully replicated in a community. It illustrates the key ingredients useful in this enterprise.

Chapter Twelve begins to examine how easy it is to misevaluate a community and how challenging it is to successfully replicate prevention programs.

Chapter Thirteen continues to explore the fragility of implementing a community prevention program. It illustrates the impact of the unpredictable and the importance of administrative support and staff continuity.

Chapter Fourteen focuses on professional and system relationships and illustrates their function in the implementation of community prevention programs.

Part Four offers a number of key considerations, which return us to the question, Why can't this business of human services help more of our children become responsible, healthy, and productive adults in today's society? Chapter Fifteen presents preliminary quantitative reports about the Rite of Passage Experience program. It also includes descriptive, qualitative data from parents, teachers, and students and discusses the limitations of the research to date.

Chapter Sixteen highlights, once again, the difficulty of providing comprehensive primary prevention strategies. It examines how policy and our systematic limitations of collaboration maintain marginal primary prevention at best.

Acknowledgments

This book would not have been possible without "people helping people." Robert Francis, Ken Freidenberg, Gene Marchand, and Ed Meincke have offered their friendship and a historical perspective on the Youth Service Bureau system. I also wish to thank my colleagues at Yale University, especially Roger Weissberg, who initially encouraged me in moving beyond practice and into the realm of writing—or, as he said, in "making a contribution" (when I thought that making a contribution meant helping people through direct practice). Rita Esposito Watson has likewise been a source of encouragement, always offering useful consultation when I needed it.

Professor Seymour Sarason urged me to write this book—and, not realizing that Professor Sarason encourages *everyone* to write a book, I did. But without his guidance, support, and review of the manuscript, I would not have written this book.

My colleagues in the Department of Youth Services deserve special praise. Their commitment and caring for others, along with their sense of humor and professional abilities, have always inspired me. They also deserve special recognition for coming to work each morning happy and cheerful and being gentle with someone who has already been up writing for four or five hours.

My deepest thanks go to my family: to my son, Michael, and to my friend and wife, Louann Virgil. Louann's review of the manuscript helped make most of it readable, and her tolerance for my late nights and early mornings at the computer was admirable beyond my ability to praise it here. Someday Michael will realize that what follows is the result of "Daddy typie typing" and will understand why "Daddy stays up all night playing computer games." More than anything else, I hope this book is worthy of him.

Glastonbury, Connecticut   David G. Blumenkrantz
June 1992

*Rite of Passage Experience© and ROPE® are copyrighted and registered marks of David G. Blumenkrantz.

The Author

David G. Blumenkrantz is director of Associates in Counseling & Training, of the Center for the Advancement of Youth, Family, and Community Service, Inc., and, since 1980, of the Department of Youth Services for Wethersfield, Connecticut. He received his B.A. degree (1975) from the State University of New York at Buffalo in psychology and his M.Ed. degree (1976) from Boston College in educational psychology. He has been a Visiting Fellow (1988) at the Bush Center for Social Policy and Child Development at Yale University. He is certified in reality therapy (1981) and parent and youth effectiveness training (1981), is a Connecticut-certified alcoholism counselor (1981) and drug counselor (1986), and is also a nationally certified alcoholism and drug counselor (1989).

Blumenkrantz has served on various boards of directors for nonprofit agencies and has been appointed to Connecticut legislative and departmental committees on teenage pregnancy, substance abuse, and delinquency prevention.

He was previously director of community resources for Justice, Inc., a community-based criminal juvenile justice organization in Hartford, Connecticut. He also served as a Youth Service officer and as chairman of the Institutional Review Board and developed the Outdoor Challenge Program for Long Lane School, Connecticut's residential and maximum-security facility for juvenile offenders.

Blumenkrantz has written articles for professional journals, newspapers, and magazines about youth and family issues, with a special focus on adolescence, substance abuse, and primary prevention. He created the Rite of Passage Experience (ROPE) and has served as a consultant and trainer to public and private human service agencies, state and local government, and education.

FULFILLING THE PROMISE OF CHILDREN'S SERVICES

PART I

Understanding Children's Services

1

Promise of Service, Practice of Failure

Several days each week, I try to arrive at work early to think and write about delivering human services from a community-based Youth Service Bureau. I attempt to describe the unfolding events that place demands on our department's resources and to think about what we are doing. The central challenge confronting the director of a Youth Service Bureau is to maintain sensitivity and a sense of proportion with respect to all the human problems we are faced with, so that we do not miss the forest for the trees—in short, to reach beyond the overwhelming, endless array of problems that youth and families face, including suicide, crime, delinquency, divorce, depression, runaway and throwaway children, a general malaise, and other crises that frequently wind up on our doorstep. People need to be comforted, and problems must be fixed or hidden from the community. The challenge is both to think and to do—to resist constant demands to be reactive and to plan for proactive prevention, to work within a bureaucratic system that has been known to extinguish the most resilient spirit in the methodical maintenance of mediocrity.

What follows are descriptions of our world—the world of a Youth Service Bureau in a middle-class suburb of 27,000 people. This is the world of a human service administrator serving, it would seem, in the capacity of a war correspondent—on the front lines, responding to the incoming artillery of social and economic change.

3

By the end of this chapter, you will know why I have to come in early.

For some, the descriptions that follow will be all too familiar. What public administrator or human service professional has not felt besieged by competing demands? These descriptions are intended to illustrate the context of the human service enterprise and put the plethora of real-life experiences in front of those unfamiliar with this reality—to bring to life, as best the written word can, how interruptions affect the job of delivering human services. For some, this presentation may be "overkill"; I hope that, for the majority, it illuminates the struggles pervasive in the delivery of human services.

The Early Bird Loses Sleep

6:45 A.M. One morning, I was continuing my attempt to create connections and order from what could only be considered unrelated service requests—a community's requests to treat teenage suicide, drug and alcohol abuse, delinquency, pregnancy, and apathy and individuals' and families' requests to fix whatever ailed their psyches. There were also requests to investigate community issues surrounding child care, welfare, and whatever else we dared examine.

I had begun to think about how these requests could be met proactively, through a comprehensive primary prevention strategy requiring intersystem collaboration. I was beginning to sift through myriad events that I hoped would create a trail, allowing me to uncover predictable problems in implementing such an intervention. I was trying to think when I was summoned to action.

7:15 A.M. A soft voice called from beyond my door.
"Hello? Hello?" The voice was almost inaudible.
I peered out of my office door, and saw Mrs. Perkins in the waiting room, grinning nervously.
"Good morning. What can I do for you?" I said, smiling, bewildered by this early visit.
"Do you have a minute?" she asked.
Another forty-five-minute minute, I thought. My smile be-

came forced. I extended my hand in greeting and led her to one of our counseling rooms.

Mrs. Perkins, along with seven other parents, had received a letter and a phone call from me earlier in the week. During the past several months, these parents' sons were reported to have participated in disruptive behavior in the community. Fighting (or, more aptly, beatings), party crashing, housewrecking, and general gang-type activities were leisure-time fun for these boys. High school students were intimidated by them. Parents whose children were threatened and beaten or whose homes were damaged did not want to "get involved." School personnel said that none of the incidents were taking place in school: "It's a community problem." To these boys' delight, everyone referred to them as a gang. On a number of occasions during the past several weeks, parents and school personnel had asked me, with anger and anxiety, "What are you going to do about it?"

Whose Problem Is This, Anyway?

What was initially a "community problem" became *my* problem. What needed a community response became my responsibility. This is typical of how systems and communities respond when confronted with a problem: they ask someone else to take responsibility and solve it. The human service system frequently serves as an "enabler" and, with great fanfare, attempts to come to the rescue. These rescue attempts serve, in part, to justify its existence. Another central challenge for those of us in human services is to empower communities and systems to accept responsibility for their own problems, but without giving the appearance of not doing our job.

The boys, who were all between sixteen and nineteen years old, were average students. Some were on the honor roll, and the majority were on the football team. I had already assembled the group several days before Mrs. Perkins came to my office. They responded predictably to my inquiries: "You've got nothing on us!" "We try to break up fights, not start them," they explained defensively, and they became even more excited when I told them that I had called all their parents that morning.

Now Mrs. Perkins was here.

"I've been worried about Pete since my divorce," she said.

"Please tell me what Pete's been doing to make you worried."

Mrs. Perkins offered a litany of difficulties: marginal grades, drinking, poor attitude, and general lack of direction had characterized Pete's immediate past. During the forty-five minute meeting, Mrs. Perkins explored a variety of possible explanations for Pete's behavior. Most plausible were Pete's absent father and poor friendship choices. I tried to shift the "explain-and-blame game" to look at the world of possible solutions while still supporting Mrs. Perkins, who was sincerely disturbed by her son's attitude and activities. I offered counseling services to her family. I also told her that our department was developing an intervention for the entire group and that I had spoken to all the boys a few days before. She thanked me and left.

8:00 A.M. The Youth Service Bureau staff began arriving for work. I generally greet my colleagues with joy and anxiety—joy for their wonderful beings, personalities, and professionalism; anxiety for their intrusion on my solitude and for the formal opening of our services. The smell of coffee floated through the offices as friendly sharing eased everyone into the day.

8:15 A.M. I returned to my pressing thoughts and my plans for responding to community problems. I have been struck by the wide variety of responses developed to resolve similar problems. Teenage drug and alcohol abuse, for example, has generated countless prevention and intervention programs. Why do certain prevention programs, employed to solve a particular human problem, take hold of a community? When a world of problems faces a community, why do people tend to focus on one and select a particular response or solution? What is particularly important to consider in thinking about the threshold where a problem meets a potential solution? Why and how does an intervention take hold in a community at a particular time? What important factors help shepherd the idea for a program into a community and allow it to grow and develop? What elements are necessary for an intervention's success? There always seem to be plenty of questions but never enough reasonable answers.

My thoughts rushed onto paper in words that seemed to fall short of explaining complex social interactions. I wrote quickly, trying to capture the best illustrations to breathe life and understanding into important social, psychological, and political phenomena. I wrote one sentence, then another.

My secretary appeared smiling at my door, carrying a stack of papers.

"Here are some purchase orders and request-for-payment forms to sign, the draft of the child care report, and the secretarial job descriptions. I'd like to speak with you when you have a minute."

"Indeed," I muttered, standing to accept this pile that would occupy my time for more than just "a minute."

I quickly sat down, casting the pile of papers to the side. Turning to write again, I strained to capture a quickly fading thought. I glanced at the pile, then back to the paper with its two short sentences at the top. The sentences looked shorter. The pile looked bigger. The thought was gone. The pile was now planted firmly in the center of my desk.

8:30 A.M. I began reviewing the purchase orders, checking financial codes and purchase descriptions, and signing my name for the millionth time. I got through the first purchase order. We would have new paper clips and pencils! My review of a request for payment for psychological consultation was interrupted by the intercom.

"It's Jennifer Snow. Do you want to talk to her?" my secretary asked. She continued indignantly, "She wouldn't say what she wanted."

I have a general rule to speak to anyone who calls: it is my responsibility as a public servant to be available to the general public. Besides, I always speak gladly to past and present clients. I have known Jennifer for about ten years. At twenty-five, she has endured the widest and wildest array of personal problems. Drug addiction, prostitution, jail, and street living are all familiar to Jennifer. I always greet her calls with delight and trepidation, always glad to hear from her but ever conscious of the potential for disaster.

"Hi, David," Jennifer moaned. "How are you?"

"Fine, Jen. How's everything with you?"

"Not too good. I'm still screwing up. I'm tired. I can't take it anymore," she said, with surprisingly little emotion.

"What are you doing now?" I asked.

"I'm in a phone booth. I think I'm real close to where you work. Can I see you now? My boyfriend beat me up last night," she whined.

"Where are you?"

She described the intersection where her phone booth was. It was indeed within a mile of my office. I took a deep breath. My secretary signaled me at the doorway, smiling, nodding at two telephone messages she held out to me. I looked at my desk: mounds of paper.

"David, David—are you still there?"

8:45 A.M. I shouldn't have looked at the telephone messages as I scurried out the door to meet Jennifer. What does the town manager want, I wondered on my way down the hall. Another general rule I have is to get back to the town manager—my boss, "the general"— as quickly as possible. I pulled out of the parking lot, thinking about what I would say to Jennifer, and drowned in a flood of thoughts and questions. Could we really do anything effective about this so-called gang? What would be the outcome of my discussion with this group of boys? with Mrs. Perkins? Is a person's desire and readiness to change important? Must a person "bottom out" first? Is there a similarity in what is needed for successful individual psychotherapy and for successful community intervention? How can we measure and know for sure the effectiveness of any particular intervention?

My thoughts evaporated as I approached the busy intersection and saw Jennifer yelling into the phone in the booth. Her arm moved rapidly, striking out, and her face signaled distress. I pulled the car up next to the phone booth. Jennifer turned, smiled quickly, and, with one last explosion slammed down the phone.

"D-a-a-a-vid, hi," Jennifer whined as she opened the car door. "How are you?"

Her voice was as sweet and sincere as could be, in sharp contrast to the anger and hostility I had seen just seconds before.

Not much has changed with Jennifer, I thought. Before I could say anything, Jennifer moaned.

"That bastard. He beat me up last night. Look at what he did to me."

Sure enough, her face was black and blue under one eye, and her lip was cut and swollen.

"Gee," I said, taking care not to incite a lengthy conversation about the beating. "What are you doing these days?" I turned the car toward the park, assuming that we would have a chat, and that this would be the end of it.

Jennifer responded with familiar tales of heroin and cocaine use, ongoing hostility with her family, no job, no money, no place to live, outstanding arrest warrants from probation violations, and growing desperation and frustration with her condition.

"How do you get by? What do you do for money? A place to sleep?" I asked, hoping to gauge her honesty by her responses.

"You know," she said sheepishly, casting her eyes downward. Then, more assured, she said, "I can get money if I want it. I know some men who I stay with. They give me money."

At the park, I opened the car window. The unseasonably warm air was refreshing, by contrast with this tale of woe.

"I'm tired of doing this bad stuff," Jennifer said, gazing out the window.

"What do you want to do?" I asked, looking to her for some reality-based solutions.

"I want to go to a hospital."

Surprised, I looked at Jennifer. In all the years I had known her, she had never mentioned hospitalization as a solution. I gazed into her dark, troubled eyes, searching for conviction and sincerity. Her stare was empty.

"I want to get help. I can't take it anymore," she said again.

Hoping to seize the moment, I returned to my office with Jennifer. I knew it would be very difficult to get her into a program, since she had no insurance and was not receiving state aid. After several calls, I was able to schedule an intake appointment for the day before Thanksgiving, one week away.

"Maybe you'll get some hot turkey with your cold turkey," I said, smiling and holding her hand. She returned my smile.

We talked about what the initial phase of rehabilitation would be like, the discomfort of withdrawal, and how she could prepare herself. Supporting and affirming her courage and wise decision, I asked her to call me every day to tell me what she was doing. I gave her bus fare, and off she went. I wondered whether she really would go to the intake. A lot can happen in one week.

I sat down again at my desk and scanned the papers before me. I needed some certainty—something from which I could get a clear sense of accomplishment, something that had closure. I signed a few request-for-payment forms. I felt great. I ordered notepads. I was confident that they would arrive. I was not so confident that Jennifer would show up for her intake appointment.

10:45 A.M. Our graduate student intern appeared at my door, smiling.

"David, can I speak with you about professional identity?"

Before I had a chance to answer her, the intercom buzzed.

"It's Ken," my secretary said.

"I'll take it," I said, beckoning the intern to look at my appointment book.

"Hi, Ken," I said. "How goes it?"

"Not bad. Listen, did you hear anything about the state changing our Youth Service Bureau reporting format?"

"Again? It doesn't surprise me. We've had our reporting format changed four times in three years. Besides, every time we ask them for data about our reports, they say we can't have any because they don't have staff to input the data! Let's get together and talk about it at lunch today. You got time?"

"We gotta eat," Ken laughed.

"The usual place at noon?" I said.

I hung up, and the intern was still looking at my appointment book.

"I don't see when I can meet with you today," she said anxiously.

"Here—why don't you see me at two? I'll go a little late to my meeting."

"Great. Thank you so much. I'll see you right after I see my clients."

"Marvelous," I muttered, returning to the stack of papers.

11:00 A.M. Signing my name is fairly automatic. I slipped into the mundane task of the bureaucratic paper shuffle, drifting off with thoughts of Mrs. Perkins, the so-called gang, Jennifer, "professional identity," Ken, and the unique institution of Youth Service Bureaus.

12:00 P.M. The last form in the pile was signed. The child care report was reviewed and had been sent back to the bureau's advisory committee for comments. Several more phone calls had been received and returned, and I was off to meet Ken for lunch—or, more accurately, I was off to lunch with Ken for a meeting.

Meetings over meals are an important ritual for several of my colleagues and me. They are opportunities to share, support, examine, laugh, cry, and complain about the myriad problems that wind up on our doorsteps. Exchanges with close and trusted colleagues are vital in sustaining a correct course of human service responses and programs, a course not altered by the winds of current funding categories but charted from points of reference on the political, social, and psychological compass.

Today's lunch was no different: several helpings of "you should have seen the case we had last week"; a side order of "look at what the state has come up with this time." Dessert is usually some tale of local political maneuvering from some constituency group. Today it was "the senior citizens want to take over the community center for themselves."

1:00 P.M. When I returned to the office, I was greeted by a familiar face, although at first I couldn't find the name to go with it. A handsome young man with blond hair, blue eyes, and a neatly trimmed beard stood to shake my hand.

"Hi, David. Do you remember me?" He grinned.

My mouth dropped open. Out of it, to my surprise, came "Jeff? Jeff Chandler, is that you?"

"Yep." He bobbed and nodded meekly, obviously pleased that I was able to remember him after about five years.

All at once his story came back to me. His case file opened from some recess in my mind. He was now twenty-two.

"How was Germany?" I asked him. "You were stationed there in the army, weren't you?"

"Yeah."

"Come in, and tell me what you've been up to. What did you do in the army?"

Sinking into a chair, he began.

"Germany was all right. I got a medical discharge about two years ago. I don't know if you've seen my mom. I got into some trouble with drugs."

My heart sank, but I tried not to lose my smile.

"Gee, that's too bad," I said. "I guess you still haven't shaken that keen interest you had in drugs and alcohol."

"No." He grinned and shook his head, with a sidelong look. "I've been kicking around for the past couple of years or so since I've been back. Odd jobs in restaurants, cooking and stuff. Got a kid by this girl who doesn't want to see me anymore because of my drug use. It's been tough."

I was silent, listening. I tried to remember more about Jeff. I felt bad, thinking that somehow we had failed him. From what he told me about himself, I could tell that he felt desperate and disappointed. I blanketed my own feelings in my counselor role and began asking what he was doing to help himself. He said he had been clean now for several weeks and had talked to another drug counselor. He wanted to believe that he was going to make it. So did I. We exchanged farewells. I told him that he was welcome back anytime and offered to help if I could. Looking back over his shoulder, he smiled and waved on his way out.

1:45 P.M. Her eyes were bulging as she raced to my side. Her cheeks were flushed, and her hands were trembling.

"I need you! I think I'm having a real emergency here!" our intern cried.

"Yes? What is it?" I asked in my calmest voice.

"I'm doing this intake on Lee Knoll, and I think she's suicidal!"

I groped for what to say, what to do.

"Where is the clinical coordinator?" I asked, fumbling, trying to shift gears for yet another unexpected event. "Oh, damn, he's at a conference," I said, answering my own question.

Conducting a suicide assessment was the last thing I thought I would have been doing that day. I waited for the intern to go on. Trial by fire, I thought. The intern nervously presented the particulars.

"Lee's mother died unexpectedly four months ago, after going into the hospital for a minor illness. Lee is nineteen. Her father is living in Arizona. The parents have been divorced for quite a while."

Testing her new professional legs, the intern began to sound detached and clinical.

"Lee was involved with a teacher at the high school, who was trying to help her," she continued. "The teacher referred her here. She's living in another town now but is planning to move in with the teacher, whose name is . . ." She looked down to decipher what she had jotted in the file.

"Mrs. Colón. Reason for referral: transitional issues, especially surrounding loss."

Looking up, the intern cried again, "I think she's going to kill herself!"

"Yes, I know. You said that." I was becoming a bit annoyed. "But what is she saying that makes you feel this way?"

"She said she attempted suicide two weeks ago but got scared and called Mrs. Colón, who took her to the emergency room. She quit her job the other day. She says she wants to be with her mother, and her life isn't worth anything."

A lump formed in my throat. How had this case gone to a student intern for an intake? How the hell hadn't we known about the suicide attempt before? Jeez, I thought, as tension welled up in my stomach.

"You did very well to consult with me," I told the intern. "She does sound like a high-risk case."

My words became more automatic as I felt my clinical hat shift comfortably into place.

"I'd like to interview her," I went on. "How do you think she'd feel about that?"

"I already asked her. She said it would be all right."

The baton was passed, and the intern was obviously relieved.

My thirty-minute interview confirmed the intern's assessment: this was a hot one. I advised her to call Mrs. Colón and see if she would transport Lee to the emergency room. Lee herself was against hospitalization.

3:15 P.M. Mrs. Colón was not convinced that Lee's situation was particularly serious, but she agreed to speak with her later in the afternoon. I had already cancelled my midafternoon appointment, and now I sat at my desk with the intern, discussing the clinical issues and playing out possible strategies and potential outcomes. We were both glum. Lee had left with a friend to wait at Mrs. Colón's house. That, at least, bought us some time.

By the end of the day, I was exhausted. I knew it was going to be a long night. The intern and I agreed to stay in touch throughout the night as we waited for the outcome of Mrs. Colón's contact with Lee and for the events that would unfold.

As I lumbered out the door on my way home, I realized that the student intern had never had a chance to speak with me about professional identity.

4:30 P.M. From my family room, I called the police to tell them that I might request them to initiate emergency transportation to a hospital if Mrs. Colón did not take Lee there. Throughout the early evening, I placed calls to three different hospital emergency rooms, to assess space and find out which psychiatrists were conducting intake assessments.

7:30 P.M. After hours of calls back and forth to Mrs. Colón, to the police, and to the student intern, Mrs. Colón was convinced that Lee's situation was serious and agreed to take her to the hospital. This was a major step. I felt somewhat relieved but apprehensive about the outcome of the hospital's assessment. Would the psychiatrist on duty confirm our assessment and hospitalize Lee, or would he or she send her home with tranquilizers? That had been known to happen.

9:30 P.M. Lee was now in the emergency room. Mrs. Colón called to keep me posted and thought that Lee would be seen within thirty minutes.

11:00 P.M. Mrs. Colón called back to update me on the situation.

"She's in with the psychiatrist," Mrs. Colón said, with a big sigh. "I didn't realize that she was this depressed. Even the crisis counselor at the school didn't think things were this serious."

"The crisis counselor at the high school saw her, too?" I tried to hide my surprise and anger that someone else had also seen Lee but not passed the information on to us before our intake.

It was late. Mrs. Colón wanted to talk. It must have seemed like an eternity for her in the hospital waiting room. I listened patiently. She is really a very dedicated teacher and a wonderful human being to care for one of her students this much, I thought.

Finally, I said to Mrs. Colón, "Lee is really very fortunate to have someone like you in her life right now. You've been very helpful in this whole thing. Thank you very much. Call me as soon as you hear anything." I hung up with the last bit of energy I could muster.

11:30 P.M. I lay on the couch, thinking about my day, which had begun almost seventeen hours before. What have we learned? What have we relearned? How can we use what we have learned to advance human services? Do people really know what it is like to work in this business? I felt myself drift off to sleep, waiting for one last call from the hospital about Lee.

1:00 A.M. The phone startled me awake. Where was I? I was still on the couch. It was Mrs. Colón.

"They've admitted Lee to the hospital. She's on her way up to a room now. The doctor said she might not have made it through the night if I hadn't gotten her here. I'm on my way home. Oh," she said, almost as an afterthought, "thank you for everything you and your department did."

"You're welcome," I said, pleased and proud, feeling energy pour into me. "We're just doing our job."

I hung up and stared at the ceiling, feeling tired but good.

Only six more hours until we start again, I thought as I got up to go to sleep.

My purpose in encapsulating this particular day was to illustrate the varied demands that confront community-based human service providers. The skeptical reader may dismiss these events as unusual, but such days do happen, more often than one might believe. I could have narrated the day when I came to work and wound up unexpectedly in Ohio, picking up a runaway, or the day I made a presentation to both houses of the state legislature on teenage substance abuse, conducted three counseling sessions, supervised a youth recreational activity, and attended a Youth Service advisory board meeting.

This particular day was clearly one when nothing of a preventive nature occurred. In this respect, it was not unusual. Educators and other human service professionals have similar days, days deluged with problems. We are all challenged to refrain from allowing them to preoccupy our thinking and our doing at the expense of our developing and implementing proactive, preventive responses. We are clearly thrust into the game of repair, and we do not even seem able to make repairs very well most of the time.

The point here is not the variety or number of service demands to which we respond but our conflict over how to spend our time—the conflict between planning or thinking about prevention and responding to the day-to-day administrative and direct service demands. A common cliché states that prevention is a luxury. In the face of ever-mounting problems of living that confront people and drain our dwindling resources, our response to people's immediate needs usually takes priority over the kind of prevention that could eliminate or diminish these growing problems.

In writing, as in the world, it is all too easy to forget the importance of prevention. It is the rare day when I feel that I have been able to deal with all the problems that have come my way. In fact, to deal with prevention—to create and implement prevention programs—is almost impossible, given the increase in service demands and the severity of problems.

Nevertheless, the particular day reported here was most satisfying, in many respects, and certainly more satisfying than endless meetings with countless people on issues far removed from the most important one—helping people directly. School personnel (especially administrators) and community-based agency staff could also describe days overflowing with service demands. We are immersed in what has essentially become systemic damage-control activity. We patch up the wounded and try to keep our communities and institutions from sinking.

Days like these, of which there are all too many, sap the spirit and foster burnout. Even worse, they create an acceptance of and even a tolerance for the status quo, which suggests that problems are intractable and that the human service system is incapable of making an appreciable difference in people's lives. Sustaining a useful level of idealism, optimism, and enthusiasm while maintaining the time and energy for thoughtful program planning, especially for primary prevention programs, is an elusive goal of the public administrator and the human service professional.

The strategies for reaching this goal and preventing burnout are as diverse as the people in pursuit of it. Although this is not a book about maintaining equilibrium in a storm of service demands and constant interruptions, I offer the following thoughts for the reader's consideration.

It is a noble thing to make the field of human services a life's work, but take care that it does not become your whole life. This is easier said than done, especially in the human services, but work should remain work. It is a part of life but not life itself. Far too often, we fail to appreciate the difference.

Before we can effectively be of assistance to others, we need to take care of ourselves and our families. We need to pursue worthy, stimulating, reenergizing outside interests. Positive leisure activities can be wonderful reenergizers and can help release toxic tension. They should be an integral part of our existence.

Develop and maintain intimate relationships with a spouse or partner and friends. We can unknowingly make our work a convenient, socially acceptable replacement for personal intimacy. Always be vigilant that you have enough support and encouragement so that you do not become addictively enmeshed with work. The drive to help others and make a significant contribution to the world, which propels many into the human services in the first place, can lead to counterproductive, unhealthy work habits—and working tirelessly for long hours is encouraged and rewarded in the human services.

Developing and sustaining collegial support aids a balanced perspective on work. The ability to let go, patience, and, when all else fails, a sense of humor are useful tools for maintaining equilibrium and proportion.

This book is about working in the human services. It is about people working with and for other people, trying to make a difference in the lives of others.

2

The Youth Service Bureau: A Model of Confusion

The origins of the Youth Service Bureau are linked to attempts to prevent juveniles from penetrating the criminal justice system. Youth Service Bureaus emerged in 1958 in Chicago and in Pontiac, Michigan, to divert children of juvenile-court age from the criminal justice system.

During the late 1960s, the war was raging in Vietnam. Unrest was brewing on college and high school campuses. The political landscape was shifting with the stress of rising social tensions. The peace and tranquility of the 1950s faded quickly with the rapid changes of the 1960s. Protest, political and sexual revolution, increased drug use, and delinquency were knocking at the door of suburbia. Communities responded by creating the Youth Service Bureaus. They were beginning to wake up and say, "Maybe we do have a problem."

The challenge confronting Youth Service Bureaus was and remains the balance between providing direct services and performing planning and coordination functions within a community, especially as they are related to prevention programs. The concept of prevention was initially developed in light of the criminal justice system. The idea was that simply keeping youth out of the justice system after they had been arrested constituted prevention. The idea of prevention did not include interventions to keep youth from developing the problems that promoted the behaviors leading to arrest in the first place. A dichotomy developed between the legal

19

view of prevention (diversion from the criminal justice system and jail) and the mental health view (prevention of mental illness, or the promotion of positive development).

One cannot understand the conflicts and problems confronting a Youth Service Bureau unless one understands how delinquency, drug and alcohol abuse, and prevention have been defined and redefined. Initially, there was a very specific and limiting definition of prevention. It was spoken of as something done to preclude youths' entry into the criminal justice system after being arrested. It did not necessarily mean stopping a youth from getting into trouble; it meant keeping a youth out of court. Judges, not unlike the rest of the community, were saying that juvenile delinquency and other problems in which youth were involved were beyond the scope of the court to remedy through incarceration or other legally sanctioned penalties or responses. The judges were also saying, less directly, "Don't bring your community problems to us. We're not social workers." If Youth Service Bureaus sought to be proactive and create prevention strategies, the orientation and substance of their responses concerned criminal justice and delinquency.

Youth Service Bureaus in Theory

Sherwood Norman's classic work, *"The Youth Service Bureau: A Key to Delinquency Prevention"* (1972), defines a Youth Service Bureau as "a non-coercive [usually] independent public agency . . . established to divert children and youth from the justice system by (1) mobilizing community resources to solve youth problems; (2) strengthening existing youth resources and developing new ones; and (3) promoting positive programs to remedy delinquency-breeding conditions" (p. 8). Norman strongly suggests that the parameters of the Youth Service Bureau should be inclusive of all youth between seven and eighteen who may eventually have contact with the justice system but for whom the authoritative intervention of the court is not needed.

There was no one prototype for a Youth Service Bureau; each community determined what the Youth Service Bureau would do to divert youth from the justice system. On the one hand, the community expected the newly created agency to "do something about these drug-crazed kids," implying a direct service capacity. Norman's parameters, on the other hand, as well as subsequent funding requirements, suggested an administrative and coordination function, which specifically excluded direct services.

Normal (1972) promoted coordination by delineating three interrelated functions: *service brokerage*, or bridging the service gap by noncoercive referral and follow-up; *resource development*, or filling the service gap by working with the community in developing new resources; and *systems modification*, or having Youth Service Bureaus constructively challenge established institutions that are affecting youth adversely, resorting to political pressure when necessary to ensure that resources and institutions are available and responsive to youths' needs.

Youth Service Bureaus in Practice

Norman's three functions were undermined by his erroneous assumption that community agencies need and want to be coordinated. In fact, there is no evidence that community, county, state, or federal agencies have now or have ever had any desire or ability to be coordinated or to work in collaboration. But this idealistic, global assumption with no basis in reality came to drive the coordination function of the Youth Service Bureaus. Norman's delineation of a coordination function was, to put the matter plainly, a disaster. It set the stage for extreme community conflict. Youth Service Bureau coordinators or directors who had no understanding of this erroneous assumption and its effects quickly became engulfed in power struggles in their communities and became part of the problem.

In some communities, newly created Youth Service Bureaus went forward with this administrative/coordination function, without firm support from the local governmental bodies that housed them. This situation caused competition and territorial disputes between the existing agencies that served youth. Unlike the other services created and provided by government (police and firefighters, engineering, health, parks and recreation), the new Youth Service Bureau was perceived as duplicating such existing services as schools and child and family agencies.

The Youth Service Bureau's mission was clouded by the language of "community coordination," and it was further entangled by the fact that its direction was to be partly determined by community representatives on an advisory board. The board would include representatives of community-based youth service agencies and schools, parents, police, and youth, who were, at best, suspicious but supportive of the newly created agency or, at worst, intent on undermining its growth and extinguishing its existence.

Again, it is important to underscore the reality that community youth-serving agencies, schools, police, parents, civic organizations, and other community resources did not want to be coordinated, and they felt bewildered (or, more likely, threatened) by the new Youth Service Bureau's "mandate" to facilitate coordination. In fact, this supposed mandate was perceived as a reflection on the adequacy and scope of existing community services.

This placed the Youth Service Bureau in a very delicate and vulnerable position. Its fate depended on five elements:

1. Overt support and empowerment from the community's power structure
2. Willingness of the existing human service community, especially the schools, to work in collaboration with one another and with the Youth Service Bureau
3. Willingness of the community, especially those representatives selected to develop the Youth Service Bureau's direction, to openly and honestly identify and evaluate community problems and resources
4. Availability of notable adult and student volunteer leaders to nurture and advise the new community agency
5. Willingness of courts and police to include the Youth Service Bureau in decision-making processes to refine and create more responsive systems and resources for youth

The Context for Leadership

The combination of these five critical elements would create the elements for a Youth Service Bureau to be born and be successful. The task of combining them fell to Youth Service Bureau staff, primarily directors or coordinators. The personality, skills, vision, ability to communicate, creativity, and knowledge of a director were inextricably linked to the success of a Youth Service Bureau. The directors had to create both a context and resources for the positive growth and development of a community's children. During the late 1960s, a unique hybrid—a mixture of minstrel, minister, and political advocate—flocked to the newly created position of Youth Service Bureau coordinator (the title of "coordinator" was more likely to be used than "director").

The Youth Service Bureau usually had a coordinator and, with any luck, some kind of secretarial assistance. In many cases, these new bureaus grew out of counseling centers, often in response to teenage delinquency and especially to teenage drug and alcohol use.

The origins of some of the Youth Service Bureaus can be traced to police departments. They, too, served as initial diversion responses to the increasing number of teenage substance users who were being arrested. Police departments began to divest themselves of the role of social worker, in which they had been caught as a result of the growth in juvenile problems. The Youth Service Bureau coordinator's role was quickly split between coordination and direct service. Police departments gladly gave these new coordinator's "crisis work" as communities tried, compassionately but covertly, to respond to the continued escalation in youth problems. The delicate balance between direct service and coordination required compliance with police requests, in the hope of producing quick and effective resolutions to youth and family crises. This would help the new coordinators gain respect and therefore access to dialogue with police and community policymakers, and to begin the process of assessment and planning. Here was the proving ground for the new coordinators. In the most simplistic terms, the community was saying, "Solve some of these crises, and then maybe we'll sit down and talk about planning." In the best situations, coordinators did get a toehold and began the process of dialogue for planning and coordination. In the worst situations, they were swamped with crisis after crisis, barely able to come up for air, let alone talk. As we will see later, developing working relationships became crucial to the success of the new Youth Service Bureau coordinators. These people were not accepted out of regard for their (nonexistent) titles or for the weight of their academic credentials but for the quality of their character.

Initial funding from federal agencies concerned with delinquency prevention, substance-abuse prevention, and mental health was channeled into the Youth Service Bureaus. The varied focus of the funding sources further divided and clouded the mission of the Youth Service Bureaus. Communities responding to the availability of funding developed grant proposals to meet funding sources' particular requirements, but what communities needed was not necessarily what funding sources were going to support. In many cases, narrow funding requirements, limited planning and grant-preparation time, and funding cycles worked against thoughtful and coordinated proposals.

Youth Service Bureau Legislation

By 1976, the State of Connecticut had developed enabling legislation to create a Youth Service Bureau system through a state and local funding partnership. Funding formulas were established, and the State Department of Children and Youth Services promulgated regulations concerning Youth Service Bureaus. *Youth* were defined as people under eighteen. A Youth Service Bureau, as defined in the Connecticut General Statute 17-443 was established for the purpose of evaluating, planning, coordinating, and implementing services for delinquent, predelinquent, and troubled youth referred by schools, police, juvenile courts, local youth-serving agencies, parents, and the youth themselves. The bureaus were authorized to provide (but were not limited to the delivery of) individual and group counseling, parental training and family therapy, work placement and employment counseling, alternative and special educational opportunities, recreational and youth-enrichment programs, and outreach programs to ensure participation and planning by the entire community for the development of youth services. The services were to divert troubled youth from the criminal justice system and provide opportunities for youth to function as responsible community members.

Youth Service Bureaus in Reality

The majority of the Youth Service Bureaus in Connecticut were established as part of municipal government, in a cost-sharing partnership. The state legislative initiative opened financial channels but did little to promulgate and support the Youth Service Bureau's coordination function at the local level. Coordination efforts were viewed with suspicion by established community agencies and institutions. Gestures intended to promote interagency communication and collaboration were rebuffed with a wide range of responses, from benign neglect to open hostility and territoriality. "We've already tried that," "It won't work," "We don't have time for this," and the favorite crippler "You don't understand" were the artillery used to stymie the newly created community-based Youth Service Bureau's coordination efforts.

Coordination functions were redirected, of necessity and for the agencies' survival. Crisis intervention, outreach and counseling, employment, Big Brother and Big Sister programs, prevention, and other supplemental services and programs were initiated to fill service gaps left, through default and neglect, by existing agencies. Gradually, services were provided directly to the community by the Youth Service Bureaus, whose actual chief reason for being was planning and coordination. Coordination and planning gave way to loose understandings and to arrangements among existing community institutions and agencies. "There are enough problems to go around" was becoming the motto of collaboration. Coordination came to mean "You do your thing and we'll do our thing, and let's not get in each other's way."

Coordination efforts continued in urban centers, where there were dozens if not hundreds of existing youth-serving institutions and agencies. Where coordination efforts clung to existence in suburban communities, Youth Service Bureau coordinators were essentially driven out. This group of early coordinators, who attempted to focus on fostering coordination, were among the first cases of burnout in the Youth Service Bureau system. For any early coordinators who survived, as for the second generation who joined their ranks as Youth Service Bureau administrators, coordination efforts went underground. Coordination strategies were discussed in secret and carried out covertly by small groups of enlightened community zealots. In no way, shape, or form were coordination efforts systematically discussed at important policy levels in communities. "There are enough problems to go around" and its opposite—"We don't have any problems in *our* community"—continued to be used (frequently in the same community) in opposition to coordinated, unified efforts to create environments that could help communities and families provide opportunities for positive youth development.

It may be an oversimplification to say that direct service demands and limited resources put coordination and prevention on the back burner. Nevertheless, is it any wonder that, in the absence of adequate resources, direct service demands always take priority over planning? Who has the desire or the time for collaborative ventures? Given the significant increase in the severity and number of youth problems today, does it make sense to overlook the necessity and benefits of primary prevention strategies? And herein lies an inherent and crippling conflict: comprehensive primary prevention strategies require coordination and collaboration among and between the major environments (family, school, community) that shape a young person's life.

Frequently, primary prevention efforts are not accepted by community leaders as directly responding to problems. Community leaders may believe that a youth worker should be hired to work directly with troubled young people; the problems of young people then become the responsibility of the youth worker. By and large, communities miss the point. This strategy divorces the community from responsible involvement with the resolution of youth problems. Primary prevention and effective attention to the problems of youth and families require a community's collective, systematic response. Such a response, by addressing the underlying causes of youth problems, eliminates the need for habitual knee-jerk reactions to daily crises. Youth Service Bureaus try to elevate the technology of primary prevention beyond simplistic responses. If "just say no" is an adequate prevention response for teenage substance use, then "just be happy" should be an adequate solution for depression. Where do I go to get my button?

3

Benefits and Challenges
of Primary Prevention

We are losing this generation—perhaps the next generation, too—as a result of society's snail's-pace reaction to rapid change. If people are really serious about primary prevention, about creating environments that present youth with opportunities to learn skills and test their abilities, and if we really want to ensure that every young person can find a place to be successful and happy in the world, then we need to do something now.

We can. We have learned much about what children and families need, how communities work, and what essential ingredients are necessary for effective, long-lasting change. But we forget so quickly. We have a body of knowledge and experience to guide us, yet everything in us helps us misevaluate what is going on and leads us to misdirect our human service efforts. Can we muster a commitment to prevention? Do we really understand what primary prevention is? Can we collaborate for the development and implementation of comprehensive primary prevention strategies?

As a society, we seem more able to respond to being clubbed over the head by a problem than to seeing the club coming—and that is not to say that we respond very well. Responses are born of critical incidents, from crises that cannot be ignored. Nuclear and toxic-waste accidents, oil spills, riots, and rampant crime get our attention. They scream for a response. Mere containment of a crisis is spoken of as "prevention." Use of the term *prevention* in this

way—to define a mopping-up operation—shifts the definition from
proaction to reaction.

A Problem of Definition

Unfortunately, *prevention* has become defined as mere response to
a problem. What is called *prevention*, however, is really an intervention that, functionally and technically speaking, should be
called *secondary prevention.*

Secondary prevention is a set of activities organized in response to some particular, existing, unwanted occurrence or behavior. Primary prevention is a set of strategies organized *before* a
defined or unwanted situation or behavior occurs. Primary prevention is directed toward promoting well-being—a positive, healthy
state. Primary prevention may mean inoculation against polio or
measles, to give one example. This medical strategy requires people
to present themselves for a shot. Quick, easy, and basically painless,
this strategy does not place much responsibility on the individuals
who deliver or receive the immunization. The inoculator must deliver good serum in the correct manner, and the population must
show up. It is a relatively passive process, which requires minimal
interaction. The effectiveness and ease of the "quick fix" method of
prevention in the medical field may lead us to believe there can be
a similar approach to problems of living.

Primary prevention strategies are directed toward the underlying causes of such problems. Primary prevention involves enhanc-
ing environments and building strengths in a general population
(as in early-childhood development programs). The Head Start program, for example, involves interactions among teachers, students,
and parents. Increased responsibility is placed on inoculators (in
this case, teachers) and on the population (in this case, parents and
young children). Each party must show up, and essential educational material must be delivered. The participating parties must
assume responsibility for actively doing something. Transmission
of values, beliefs, and skills is critical to the success of this primary
prevention effort.

Moving Beyond Denial

To fully embrace and employ the concept of prevention, one must come to grips with the possibility that uncomfortable and perhaps embarrassing events not only are likely but also are already occurring. Initial reports about Chernobyl, Three Mile Island, and the Exxon-Valdez oil spill, for example, were either denied or, when finally acknowledged, distorted to give the impression that things were under control—by means of "prevention" (preventing the spread of the oil spill or the radiation).

The recent ambivalence toward and reluctance to pay attention to the spread of AIDS in our country reflects a general tendency to underrespond, to fail to anticipate and understand or accept how a sequence of events can lead to an epidemic. As Randy Shilts (1987) points out, "AIDs did not just happen to America—it was allowed to happen by an array of institutions, all of which failed to perform their appropriate tasks to safeguard the public health" (p. xxii). Prevention is built from the acceptance that this is not a perfect and wholly functional world, and that we are not a perfect species. It is a safe bet that young people will continue to have serious problems growing up and assimilating to the sanctioned adult world. We need to begin focusing our attention on important questions: Given the societal problems we have today, how do we begin to think about comprehensive primary prevention strategies? What is missing from the experience of people, especially from young people's development, that should inoculate them against such societal problems as drug and alcohol abuse?

Rediscovering Prevention

How can we move beyond "rediscovering" the same old problems and move toward proactive, primary prevention approaches? Consider teenage substance abuse, which was reported among youth long ago. Recent accounts of both teenage and adult alcohol and drug abuse would lead us to believe that it is a recent phenomenon. In our desire to represent it as a modern affliction of youth, we continue to overlook its long history as a major social issue for youth and adults, an issue that precipitated a similar sequence of earlier responses, including education, social action, prohibition, and prosecution. (During the past several decades, each successive presidential administration has declared, with all kinds of fanfare, a "war on drugs").

History texts abound with illustrations of and anecdotes about early America's battle with the bottle. The temperance leagues of the 1800s responded to concerns about alcohol. Records of "spirits" traded in this period reveal a per-person consumption of alcohol almost double that of today. In fact, there are reports of a youth-initiated movement called the Cadets of Temperance, which appears to have been a forerunner of the current Students Against Drunk Driving program. In 1914, Frances M. Morehouse, supervisor of high school teaching at the Illinois State Normal University, discussed widespread inhaling of chloroform and the practice of shooting heroin and cocaine among high school students. Written history tells us that adults since the 1820s have been convinced that the velocity of social change was disrupting traditional harmony and having a tremendously negative effect on youth. All in all, we have yet to appreciate the fullness of human experience as it concerns adolescence or substances that alter one's perception of the world.

The fact is that comprehensive primary prevention is more about creating systems change than about producing individual change. Again, it is crucial that we begin to identify what is missing from people's experience, what allows and actually promotes problems. Can we expose those missing elements? Can we replace them through corrective strategies? To be sure, these are no easy questions, but answering them is fundamental in developing strategies that can intervene and inoculate individuals against the problems of living.

Our failure to use existing knowledge and preferred practice in the creation and implementation of primary prevention programs is complex. More than anything else, it is a function of our continued failure to evaluate situations and to work together. This failure stems in part from our mistaken belief that all families have two parents, one male and one female, who provide for their children and guide them on a simple, well-charted course to adulthood—parents cast in the mold of Ozzie and Harriet Nelson, or Ward and June Cleaver. Our comfortable fantasies picture communities built from interconnections among their citizens. In these communities, churches and schools complement the family's support of children on their path to spiritual, moral, and educational adulthood. Children are characterized by their prosocial behavior and by beliefs consistent with the community's and society's standards. Time stands still. Nothing changes in these idyllic communities produced and directed by Rod Serling and only seen on "The Twilight Zone."

When we expose these fantasies for what they are, we see a more unsettling picture. Perhaps it shakes our deep-seated beliefs about the society and the country we have created. Our first reaction after acknowledging the problems of our young people has usually been to seek a culprit, someone to blame. We spend an inordinate, unproductive amount of time focusing the blame for "failure" on the central institutions of our society: the family has failed to stay together; schools and communities have failed to support the academic skills and positive social development of our young people; religion has failed to fulfill the spiritual needs of our children and youth. Each of these problems is more about societal change than about individual change. Focusing blame on the family, schools, and religion does little to help us understand what we need to do. Clearly, our failures lie more in our central institutions' unwillingness to acknowledge and accept a changing world and in their inability to collaborate in developing appropriate, productive responses.

Denial of change, denial of problems, a focus on failure, and a preoccupation with blame are crippling our country. These habits set the stage for our failure to understand and use existing primary prevention concepts and practices. Social science's strategies for delivering primary prevention interventions are far more complicated— and, so far, much less effective—than medical science's interventions for combating disease. If there is anything we know, however, it is that primary prevention, in the long run, is the most cost-effective and productive thing we can do. But nobody said it would be easy.

Somewhere over the Waterfall: A Fable

Once upon a time (as all good fairy tales should begin), the local community services, the school system, and the state and federal youth-serving agencies were all walking through the woods—not together, of course.

The cries of young children brought these groups together on the banks of a swiftly running river. All stood gasping at the sight of a child caught in the current and plunging over a waterfall.

Quickly, the physical education teacher from the local school system—under direct supervision of the departmental chairperson, and after careful consideration from the building principal, who first received administrative approval from the superintendent— jumped into the river to rescue the child.

An intervention occurred. A precedent was set.

The child was brought to the shore, and it was apparent to all that he was not breathing. All the children gathered around and screamed, "Do something!"

The nurse from the community service agency knelt by the child's side and prepared to administer artificial respiration. The school principal quickly stepped up and said, "Hold it right there. I believe that the child is in our jurisdiction. We rescued him, and he is now our responsibility."

The nurse, bewildered, stopped what she was doing.

The principal looked around and asked, "Is there any school staff member who knows how to perform artificial respiration?"

No one responded. All was still.

Just then, there was a loud shriek from the children: "Look! Look! Come quick! Another child is about to go over the waterfall!"

Before anyone could say anything, the physical education teacher was back in the water, dragging another child to shore. Everyone in the crowd moved to the banks and, together, carried the next boy to safety.

Fortunately, he was still alive.

Time passed, and all the adults were firmly ensconced at the bottom of the waterfall, positioned and ready. They were amazed at the number of children who were going over the waterfall. Fortunately, there were many adults, representing many organizations, who cared. They all wanted to do something.

Precedence was established and, under the school's jurisdiction, the physical education teacher was able to rescue about 50 percent of the children—at first. But he got tired, and then he was busy preparing to teach a new requirement—AIDS education—to the children, and so he was unable to respond as quickly as he had responded before.

The federal people said that they would bring money and try to help the exhausted teacher out, if the state would plan an appropriate response.

A committee was formed.

State workers met for months, conducting open forums with many agencies and systems, and decided that the long drop over the waterfall was decreasing the chances of the children's survival. They said that an adequate and appropriate response should begin at the top of the waterfall, before the children reached that spot.

And so the governor decreed, through official proclamation and with much fanfare, that everyone had to move to the top of the waterfall and "wage war on this scourge, which is killing our children." The federal agencies came forth with money but with the stipulation that the private sector contribute 75 percent toward the cost of the program. State agencies were responsible for channeling the federal monies, but they had a stipulation that "strongly encouraged" all the agencies to develop a coordinated response.

Meanwhile, back at the riverbank, the children continued to plunge over the waterfall, and the physical education teacher was far behind in teaching the required AIDS curriculum.

More adults began to gather on the bank. A grass-roots organization of parents stepped forward and asked the agency professionals if any of them were going up to the top of the waterfall to stop the children from going over the edge.

The people from the school board said that they had been rescuing the children for a long time and were too overloaded with other demands. They could not go up to the top of the waterfall.

The people from the community service organization said that they could not do it alone but would go up to the top of the waterfall with the parents.

Together, the parents and the community service people climbed to the top of the waterfall, where they began to rescue the children still coming downriver. The current was very fast at the top of the falls, which made rescue very difficult and dangerous. Still, the parents and the community service group worked very hard and rescued more than 50 percent of the children. The school people pulled out many of the remaining children, who had gone over the falls.

Of course, most of those children had already drowned.

After some time, the school people, seeing the success of the group at the top of the falls, offered to coordinate their efforts. They hired an administrator and a staff to oversee the program. The parents were delighted that they did not have to be involved anymore. The community services people were thanked for their efforts and told that they were not needed anymore.

But more and more of the children were still going over the falls, and the school people were getting tired of pulling so many out of the river.

As luck would have it, the students began to talk with the school system. They said that there was a spot upriver where the children were entering the river.

"Wouldn't it be most helpful to stop the children from going into the river in the first place?" one child asked innocently.

"It is very far upriver to that spot, and we don't know if that would work. Besides, we are too busy here pulling the children out of the river," a school person answered.

"Oh, please—do something!" cried one of the children. "So many of our friends are being lost."

Hearing the children's pleas, a group of parents, the community services organization, and a group of the children, along with a group of caring teachers, set out on their own on a journey upriver. The children showed the adults where their friends were entering the river.

Together, they all worked to prevent more children from entering the river. From that point on, no more children went over the waterfall.

That is primary prevention.

PART II

A Comprehensive Intervention

4

The Process of Prevention

It would be a glaring simplification of the problems that society in general and youth in particular face to assume that one program could successfully provide a solution. In fact, however, we have quite ignorantly been accepting and embracing the "one slogan" or "one program" approach for decades. The slogan "just say no" is offered as a solution to teenage drug and alcohol abuse, along with dozens of nicely packaged and widely marketed drug and alcohol programs.

Historically, we have focused on "sole source" and "quick fix" solutions. A similar rationale—that one person with one pill can solve our problems—got us into the drug and alcohol dilemma in the first place. We go to the physician for medication to cure our ills. If we do not get pills or a shot, we are bewildered and angry that we have not been treated properly. It is no wonder that we look toward one source—in this case, primarily education and the schools—to dole out the "pill" to fix youth's problems, and we expect results immediately.

It should be clear that human problems do not yield quickly to slogans and "quick fix" solutions. There are no permanent, static, "cookbook" formulas that solve human problems. Strategic interventions, born of an ongoing process of exploration and community collaboration and employed along a continuum of opportunities, have the best chance to be useful. We need to expose those elements of a person's experience whose absence contributes to problems, and we must provide a series of ongoing, supportive strategies, developed and implemented through collaboration by diverse representatives of the community. If we can do this, then we can be collectively responsible for helping young people learn a healthy, socially appropriate manner of living. We can do things to help nurture and support children and families. In short, if there are solutions (and, again, this is a tentative proposition), they result from people's caring about and helping other people, especially young people on their journey to adulthood.

One primary prevention strategy on which we will focus in this chapter is the Rite of Passage Experience (ROPE). This strategy is conceptualized and employed as a community intervention that sees one missing element—rituals of initiation—as historically important but currently absent in individuals' and in our culture's experience. Although curriculum materials grounded in developmentally appropriate content do exist in this intervention, it is more about an ongoing *process* than about a static set of procedures that make up a *program*.

It would be a mistake to view this strategy as a program without also focusing on its use as a process that involves wide representation of the community in assisting with young people's passage from childhood to adulthood. It involves parents, schools, and community agencies supporting youngsters' transition from childhood to adulthood while teaching essential skills and beliefs.

The idea that this intervention—ROPE—is a process, not a content contained in a program, has often been misunderstood, downplayed, or ignored. Nevertheless, the Rite of Passage Experience, as conceived, is embedded in the community. It serves as a vehicle to transmit and preserve the essential beliefs, attitudes, and skills that a community values and wishes to foster in future generations.

No "Quick Fix" for Problems of Living

In pursuit of the "quick fix," we have become obsessed with the search for a "final product," desperately seeking one activity as a "pill" for human problems, rather than accepting that viable, effective responses emerge and continue from an ongoing process of discovery and adaption. As a brief example, consider the almost complete failure of psychotherapy with the symptoms of alcoholism. On their own, brief or long-term hospitalization, medication, and time-limited psychotherapies are all mostly inadequate. They are finite events, which have an ending and an expected outcome of symptom reduction and success; yet ongoing participation in Alcoholics Anonymous (AA) appears to be the single most effective treatment, one that helps produce discoveries in individuals for their continued adaption to life. AA helps focus participants on the ongoing process of daily living. Recovery from alcoholism is never complete; people are always in process of recovery. Recovery is not a finite, final product but rather a human interchange grounded in the Alcoholics Anonymous twelve steps and traditions. Part of why AA works *is* that recovery is an ongoing process that involves (1) owning up to a kind of immaturity—"I am an alcoholic"—as a way of becoming more mature, and hence, renouncing one condition (alcoholism) for a better one (sobriety); (2) taking on obligations and responsibility, not only for oneself but also for others; (3) accepting beliefs and outlooks that are held not only by those in AA but also by the community and society at large; (4) developing a sense of belonging to a mission for transcending one state (alcoholism) and moving on to another (sobriety); (5) accepting that one is always in a process of recovery (living).

We may just have to face and accept the fact that human problems, which have precipitated a plethora of program responses from countless human service agencies, are unsolvable—unsolvable in the sense that solutions do not come wrapped in tidy little packages tied with a theoretical "bow."

For the same reasons that AA is useful in the alcoholism recovery process, rituals of initiation hold promise for communities in helping young people (1) renounce one status (childhood) for another one (adulthood); (2) grow in understanding of obligations toward and responsibility for others; (3) accept the beliefs of the adult community and learn the skills necessary for survival and success; (4) tap into a supportive community network that will help them cross the threshold into adulthood; and (5) embrace the human interaction that is the ongoing process of living.

Rites of Passage

Rituals of initiation or rites of passage, once a central cultural experience in families and communities, have been forgotten. Today's teenagers, lacking meaningful attachments, are finding ritual introductions to adulthood that are in conflict with society. Consider how the following vignette illustrates youths creating their own rite of passage. Is this a modern-day rite of passage?

> The youths sit warming their hands around a fire. Their eyes shift to catch one another's gaze. They speak softly. It is time to cross over the threshold into the adult world.
>
> The sound of brush moving along the nearby trail puts an end to their soft, nervous chatter. They look at one another. They rise. Casting aside a jug of wine, flipping away half-smoked cigarettes, they jump from behind the bushes and confront a couple gliding arm in arm along the park path. Knives flash in the moonlight. In a moment, it is over. Money changes hands. Jewelry is tugged from wrists. A necklace breaks and falls to the ground.
>
> The youths retreat back into the night. They have what they came for. They have crossed the threshold. They have shared a ritual. They are forever transformed.

Indeed, this vignette could illustrate a negative rite of passage.

In the absence of any clearly sanctioned rite of passage, there will be a void. Too many teenagers today are filling the void with destructive, chaotic, asocial attempts to find support in and connections to the adult world. The complexities of modern society make the formulation of a cultural rite of passage difficult. Again, this challenges us to assemble broad representation from the community, to create a meaningful, culturally relevant, developmentally appropriate rite of passage.

A modern-day ritual of initiation, such as the Rite of Passage Experience (ROPE), provides activities in a ceremonial process. When linked together, they promote good physical health and nutrition, develop decision-making and problem-solving skills, build competencies, increase self-esteem, and, most important, enhance the support systems that help strengthen links among and between schools, family, community, and peers. Another distinguishing feature of this rite of passage is its development and delivery through a community process, thus establishing greater community commitment to and responsibility for the growth and development of children. There is adequate coaching and training of youth to help prepare them for productive adult roles. A clear and challenging path engages both youth and adults in the transmission of important prosocial behaviors and beliefs during the transition from childhood to adulthood.

In the following chapters, I will zero in on a concrete approach that takes primary prevention seriously. This strategy is undertaken as a community intervention. Therefore, it requires the involvement of as much of the community as possible, including parents, teachers, community counselors, business people, clergy, and others. It is not a panacea or a "quick fix" for the complex problems inherent in raising healthy children. The foundation of the strategy rests on the historical but recently forgotten concept of rituals of initiation, or rites of passage.

Rites of passage once served humanity in many ways—across varied cultures, and for millennia. All premodern societies accorded primary importance to the idea and practice of initiation ceremonies, which provided an important benchmark, a link along the continuum from birth to death. If rites of passage were so important to all previous cultures, what is the impact of their absence on today's society and on youth in particular? What would be the impact if, for some mysterious reason, funerals or weddings suddenly disappeared?

The Rite of Passage Experience illustrates one type of primary prevention, which has been employed successfully and received enthusiastically by communities, parents, and children. It demonstrates how a community collaborates to do something for and with children that can help them move from childhood to adulthood. A distinguishing feature of the Rite of Passage Experience is its focus on empowering the community to engage in a dynamic process for developing, expanding, modifying, and implementing a primary prevention strategy.

Another promising approach comes from the Social Development Research Group at the University of Washington School of Social Work (Hawkins, Haggerty, & Catalano, in press). Called "TOGETHER! Communities for Drug-Free Youth," it attempts to directly mobilize a community in a planning process for reducing substance abuse. It promotes an admission of problems (helping a community move beyond denial) by identifying thirteen risk factors whose presence promotes and is a predictor of youth problems. Like ROPE, it is a primary prevention effort that focuses on fostering collaboration and on empowering the community to promote positive development in young people. (Other approaches are discussed in Price, Cowen, Lorion, and Ramos-McKay, 1988.)

I encourage the reader to think about what has to happen in order for the activities described in the next three chapters to occur. What community resources (staff, facilities, insurance, equipment, and the like) must be committed before such an endeavor can be successful? Is it any wonder that communities, caught up in responding to crisis after crisis, forgo the complex, difficult task of undertaking comprehensive primary prevention?

5

॰॰॰

Applying
an Ounce of Prevention

It is early evening. Dusk is yielding to the darkness looming under swiftly moving clouds. One hundred parents and their eleven- and twelve-year-old-children, in their final year of elementary school, congregate excitedly in the junior high school cafeteria.

One by one, the children disappear. They are guided to their secret meeting place. Through darkened hallways illuminated by candlelight in the basement of the school, they walk with community elders, shrouded in mystery. The children's excited chatter is overcome by a hush of anxiety.

In groups of twelve, they sit on the floor in a circle around a small candle. Captivated by the story of a youth in a far-off land, they are about to go on their rite of passage. Mystery and tension build as the children watch a videotape about rituals of initiation and the community elders introduce them to the challenge of their rite of passage, which lies before them.

While the children's attention is shifted to the importance of this period in their lives, their parents are receiving an orientation and are advised of their responsibilities during their children's Rite of Passage Experience.

The Children's Experience

A soft touch on the shoulder. A beckoning look. Another child is summoned away from his parents by a community elder. Two by two, the children are taken to an alcove in a hallway outside the cafeteria.

"This is a special evening for you," a guide tells two students in a mysterious yet gentle tone. Their wide eyes are riveted on the unfamiliar elder. "You are about to embark on a very important journey. A journey that will take you through dangerous territory on your passage from child to adult. Tonight you will be initiated. You will participate in a special ceremony to mark a point of transition. You must listen carefully. Your life depends on it. Come with me now."

The two students cast uncertain glances at each other as they both turn, hoping to catch the eyes of their parents. They are nudged toward a doorway. Following their guide, they move carefully through the darkness. Candles flicker against the stairwell. The students cling to the rail as they descend to the basement of the unfamiliar school. They sense acutely a soft, mysterious rhythm drifting up from a long corridor at the bottom of the stairs. They are led to a classroom, which is dark except for a single candle on the floor. They are directed to join their fellow students, seated in a circle around the candle. Faces are illuminated ever so faintly in the darkness. Twelve children sit in silence. The mysterious rhythm of the drums continues as a community elder reads a tale about another child on the passage to adulthood: "The woods were dark and alive with the mysterious sounds of the night. A fourteen-year-old, SumJay, huddled close to the small fire. With bare back and wearing only a loincloth, SumJay shivered in the chill of the night air."

The children huddle closer, attentive to the tale, clinging to the spoken word, trying to make sense of this strange and startling experience. The elder's reading is deliberately slow and methodical, pausing to allow the subtle meaning of the tale and the penetrating rhythm of the drums to shift the students' attention. They are captured by the moment. The elder reads on: "SumJay's thoughts were of the night, the first of several nights, to be spent in the Roaring Woods. Here, SumJay would attempt a challenge on the passage to adulthood. A rite of passage. Viki, SumJay's father, and many elders before them had been chilled by the sounds of the night in the

Roaring Woods. Here, they had all been taught by their elders to survive in the woods. Now it was SumJay's turn."

The elder peers deep into the children's eyes and concludes the story of this youth's journey.

When the story ends, there is stillness. Slowly, the elder raises his arm. The wide eyes of the children follow. Finally, the arm stops, pointing toward a large television. The children's eyes fix on the screen.

"You are in the company of community elders." The voice of a figure appearing on the screen leaps into the children's hearts. The figure, shrouded in a strange mask, continues:

"They are here, as your parents are, to prepare you for an important journey. To initiate you into your Rite of Passage Experience."

The children exchange glances, giggling softly.

"You are at a crossroads in your life. No longer totally children, yet certainly not adults. You need to prepare for crossing the threshold from childhood to adulthood. The elders with you tonight—your parents, teachers, and the community—are here to help teach and support you on this journey to adulthood. It is a perilous journey, full of traps and difficulties.

"During the next seven weeks, you will become involved at school in a journey that will teach you the important skills, beliefs, and attitudes that the adult community expects from you. Together, in small groups, you will be on your Rite of Passage Experience. Rites of passage are thousands of years old. Here is an example of a rite of passage, seen in the movie *The Emerald Forest*."

The rite of passage of a young boy from an indigenous South American tribe is dramatically depicted on the screen. Drums beat loudly in the background as tribal elders dance around the trembling young boy. The campfire reveals dread on the boy's face. Ants cover the boy's body as he shakes uncontrollably. The elders continue to dance in the glow of the fire.

The scene quickly shifts. It is morning. The tribe's medicine man is holding the boy in his arms. They are standing waist-deep in water. The tribe stands quietly on the surrounding banks.

"The boy is dead. The Man is born," the medicine man chants, dunking the boy in the fashion of a baptism.

The children once again exchange glances. There are no giggles.

The face in the mask reappears.

"What you have just seen is an example of an ancient ritual. A ceremony to mark for that young boy and his tribe, his community, that he has entered the world of adulthood. Let us hear now what a very learned man, Dr. Joseph Campbell, says about rites of passage."

Scenes from the public television program "The Power of Myth and Ritual," featuring Bill Moyers's interview with Campbell, depict more ancient rites of passage. Campbell's commentary on the meaning and importance of rites of passage serves as the narration for an African scarring ceremony, graphically shown.

The children's eyes are fixed on the television. The children may be uncertain of the exact meaning of Campbell's words, but they are sure they are in for some serious business.

The man in the mask returns.

"Some of you understand what Dr. Campbell has said. You are farther along on the path to adulthood than your friends. That is all right.

"During your Rite of Passage Experience, you will be engaged in a series of challenges. These challenges will help you learn many important things essential to your survival in the adult world. You will all learn a lot. The most important thing is to accept all challenges. To try what you think you may not be able to accomplish. This is the first important lesson. What you do not try, you cannot accomplish. What you cannot accomplish, you cannot learn from."

The television set booms, "They climb as if with boulders on their shoulders." Tom Brokaw's familiar voice narrates the climb of the tallest cliff in the world, El Capitán, by a paraplegic man and his friend and aide. "Undaunted by 105° heat and howling winds, they climb straight up. For seven days . . ."

This excerpt from the "NBC Evening News" puts a dramatic capstone on the students' orientation to their Rite of Passage Experience. Tom Brokaw's description of the climbers' efforts as "the most difficult and rewarding challenge in modern sports" is invigorating, filling the students with a sense of spirit, a belief that almost anything may be possible.

"Wow!" one student exclaims.

"Are we going to do that?" another asks expectantly.

The students await the next word from the elders.

"You'll find out when you get there," the elder offers, to the students' anxious dissatisfaction.

The Parents' Experience

Back in the cafeteria, the parents, invited to this important meeting by the superintendent of schools, the children's principal, and the director of the town's Youth Service Bureau, engage in a presentation about the meaning and purpose of rites of passage. They watch the same videotape about rites of passage that their children view. In addition, they are given a detailed explanation of the Rite of Passage Experience, in which their children will participate during the next several months. This community intervention requires the parents' participation, for which they are recruited during this orientation.

After the last child has been taken away, I stand before the assembled group. The room is abuzz with the friendly banter of seventy-five to one hundred parents. I nervously clear my throat, in hopes of attracting attention. In my most ceremonial and solemn tone, I begin.

"If you have not already noticed, your children are gone. We have taken your children."

The talking quickly ceases as parents nervously peer around the room, eyeing one another with mounting concern.

"They are beginning their journey through adolescence," I continue. "They are in the presence of community elders who are initiating them into the Rite of Passage Experience."

They are completely captivated. Tension fills the air, and I pause to extract the most from the moment. I look at their faces. They wait expectantly for my next words. I playfully deliver the punchline.

"But don't you worry," I say. "They'll all be going home with you tonight."

A long groan and laughter break the tension.

"This is an important evening for you and your children," I continue, switching to a more professional tone. "Your children are receiving information about the Rite of Passage Experience. As you know, this is the period of your child's life—adolescence—for which you have all waited with varying degrees of dread and uncertainty. Most of you would like to see your children go to sleep one night and wake up the next morning as adults."

Laughter ripples through the audience.

"During the next several years, you and your children will be presented with many challenges. Growing up is difficult in today's complex world."

The parents nod in agreement.

"Children benefit from a broad safety net of support and teaching during these important years of their development. The school, the community, and you, parents, need to form this safety net. To do this, we call upon the ancient tradition of rites of passage."

I move to an explanation of the historical, anthropological, and sociological reason for rituals of initiation.

"In all premodern cultures, the rite of passage was a central and important ceremony. It served to ensure the transmission of important beliefs, behaviors, and skills essential to the survival of the tribe or culture. Out of respect and understanding for the importance of this ritual, we have developed a modern-day version called Rite of Passage Experience, or ROPE.

"What would the world be like if there were no rituals or ceremonies surrounding death, birth, or marriage? Funerals, birthdays, and weddings offer communities and individuals a way to mark that something different has happened—that a transformation or change has taken place.

"Right now, your children are watching a videotape that is somewhat intimidating. It shows graphic scenes from the movie *The Emerald Forest*, about a young boy's rite of passage. Also, Joseph Campbell and Bill Moyers discuss the purpose of rites of passage. In a moment, you will see the same video. We expect your children to have many questions about their rite of passage.

"No, we will not scar them or engage them in any ancient

tribal ceremony, like the one you will soon see in the video. Although, if you wish, for a small fee, we would be happy to oblige,'' I offer. Laughter erupts once again.

"We wanted to bring you together with your children for this orientation or initiation into the Rites of Passage Experience, as a way of shifting your and your children's attention. This is an important time. Something different is about to happen. You and your children have important responsibilities.

"Please let your children know that they will be safe during their Rite of Passage Experience and that you and their teachers, school personnel, and the community are there to help prepare them for their transition into the adult world. Tell them that we are all here to support them on their difficult and important journey through adolescence. Tell them you love them. Tell them we all care.

"We will now view the videotape that your children are seeing right now. After the video, you will see a slide presentation about the first part of the Rite of Passage Experience. It is important that you not tell your children what will happen during their Rite of Passage Experience. If they ask, please tell them that they will find out when they get there."

The room darkens, and the videotape runs. It is followed by the slide presentation about the Rite of Passage Experience. The slides present material on each of thirteen sessions, illustrating twenty-one hours of the strategy comprising the first phase of the three-phase, six-year process of this modern-day rite of passage. Certain sessions are presented from the perspective of the parents' role. Several sessions require parents' interaction with their children at home, while others require actual parental participation.

"As we have been saying all evening, you need us and we need you in order to help your children through adolescence. This first phase of the Rite of Passage Experience is intended to teach your children important skills—decision making and problem solving, understanding peer pressure and what it means to be part of a group, and how groups work. They learn about trust and cooperation while gaining a sense of importance and power, which ultimately helps to increase their self-esteem.

"These thirteen sessions form the building blocks to the second and third phases of this modern-day rite of passage. Let me tell you a bit about the second phase.

"But first, let me clear up a long-standing misconception about parents, children, and junior high school. For a long time, parents believed that once their children left elementary school, the parents' involvement in school was virtually over or certainly curtailed. Schools supported this belief by telling parents, 'Your child really doesn't want you near the school.' Incredible as it may seem, parents obey their children's plea and stay away from school!

"To a certain extent, parents begin the critical period of separation by removing themselves from a large part of their children's life all at once. But, please, make no mistake—the period of early adolescence is a time for the beginning of parent-child separation. However, your children, the school, and the community need you to continue providing a strong influence, guidance, support, and supervision. Children need to feel that there will be a place in the adult world that can be rewarding and fun.

"Our job is to ensure that each of these adolescents finds productive, positive, and fun ways to utilize free time. Our challenge is to guide these impressionable youngsters into positive leisure-time activities, activities that require them to learn a skill in order to perform well, something that they can accomplish, and from which they will feel a sense of satisfaction. It may be a sport, a hobby, a craft, computers, or some science project like rocketry or chemistry. The world is full of these kinds of opportunities. But we must put them within our children's reach. The community, the school, and the parents must expect young people to become involved in something positive, especially after school.

"During the thirteenth session of the Rite of Passage Experience, your children will fill out contracts with their ROPE guides. With our guidance, they will review this booklet."

I hold the booklet up.

"It contains over seventy-five different opportunities in which students may participate, opportunities for them to learn skills in productive activities. They will be asked to pick three different activities with which they would like to experiment when they get to junior high school. Many, many activities are offered in the after-school programs sponsored by the school and other community-based agencies, such as the Youth Service Bureau and the Recreation Department. There are Little League and church activities. Again, our job, our challenge as part of the second phase of this process, is to guide children to experiment with and find satisfaction in these positive activities.

"Also, as part of this second phase of the rite of passage, we recognize the importance of parents' participation in the functioning of the junior high school. A wide variety of important tasks have been identified by the school principal, teachers, and other parents. Your participation in these tasks is essential. We need to harness the energy, talents, and resources of parents in order to enhance children's school experience. Next year, you will be asked to get involved with your school. Do it! We need you. We cannot educate your children in today's difficult and complex world without you. I cannot overstate the importance of this.

"Now, back to ROPE. The Rite of Passage Experience is the first part of our journey. Your participation in several of the sessions is critical. Now is the time to sign up. We ask you *not* to sign up for a session that includes your child. Here are the designated times."

I hold the sign-up sheets aloft as the parents move to the front of the room. Within a minute, almost all the parents are talking excitedly around the table with the sign-up sheet on it. I retreat into the background and exhale, releasing my tension and excitement.

Parents and Children Share an Initiation

A commotion in the hallway shifts my attention to the children waiting outside. The children rejoin their parents in a state of bewilderment, anxiety, and excitement. Questions mount about their own rite of passage and the responsibilities that their impending adolescence and adulthood will bring. They are beginning to cross the threshold. They are beginning to be transformed. They will be in the presence of community elders. They drive off into the night with their parents.

This parent-child initiation into a modern day rite of passage sets the stage for the community intervention. It directs attention to the importance of rituals of initiation and to how parents, the community, and the schools are responsible for guiding youth on the perilous journey from childhood to adulthood. It gives parents some preliminary skills for helping their children. It also transmits the following messages to both parents and youth:

1. The transition from childhood to adulthood is difficult.
2. To transcend the difficulties of adolescence successfully and become a happy, healthy adult, it is essential to learn certain skills.
3. To transmit the essential knowledge and skills effectively to children, the parents, the schools, and the community must work together to provide a modern-day rite of passage.
4. To learn these essential skills, a child can participate in the Rite of Passage Experience.

Parents and children alike are engaged in a dramatic and emotional process. The evening presentation is designed to raise anxiety in children and then place them immediately back with their parents for comfort, support, and teaching. Community elders, school personnel, and Youth Service Bureau counselors are identified, to show that different kinds of support and guidance are available to children on their passage from childhood to adulthood.

Inherent in this strategy is the community's consensus and its overt agreement on the following points:

1. In the world today, we have problems socializing and bringing up the next generation.
2. Together, we have embraced a strategy that can help us raise our children.
3. The strategy utilizes a structured, multiphase process that occurs over a number of years and requires considerable effort and participation on the part of the entire community.
4. Young people grow up developing healthy and positive beliefs, values, and behaviors when communities provide opportunities for them to learn essential skills while gaining a sense of competence. Strong support is essential during the period of "awakening" or transition to adulthood.

5. The strategy does not promise a "quick fix."
6. As a community, we will make modest resources available to support the implementation of the Rite of Passage Experience.
7. Enhancement and coordination of the major environments within which youths develop (family, school, peers, and community) is critical in ensuring that opportunities exist for their involvement.

The strategy of this community intervention, using the ancient tradition of rites of passage, recognizes the difficulty that society currently has in raising the next generation. By employing this strategy, we marshal all available and appropriate community resources to help in that task.

6

The Rite of Passage Experience

The door to the sixth-grade classroom swings open. In walk four community elders, guides from the community's Youth Service Bureau. The students' faces offer glimmers of recognition.

"Hey!" a student blurts out. "You were there at the school last night." The student's voice trails off with the realization that it is time for the rite of passage.

"We have come for your children," one of the guides announces to the teacher, who is already prepared to discharge the students in the predetermined groupings used during the orientation the night before. The class sits gazing in silence as the guides call out each student's name.

"Brown, Lisa Brown . . . Smith, Charles Smith . . . Miss Brown, Mr. Smith, please come to the door and stand over here by Guide Stan."

The two students rise slowly. They look at each other, then to the rest of the class. The rest of the class returns nervous smiles and vacant stares to the students now standing by the door. The roll call continues. The room buzzes with anticipation as the guides call their charges. One by one, students answer the call and line up by the door. The first half of the class is standing by the door. Twelve students are escorted out of the classroom by two guides. The roll call begins again for the rest of the class. Another twelve students are taken.

The Initiation Continues

The first group is escorted down the hall into a small, cloistered part of the library. The second group remains in the classroom. Both groups receive the same one-hour initiation into the Rite of Passage Experience.

The students are asked to sit on chairs arranged in a circle.

"Are we going to go on a hunt for our survival?" John, a student, asks playfully. All the students giggle nervously.

"In a way, we are going on a hunt, which may help all of you survive in the future," Stan responds, his voice gentle and reassuring.

The students refocus their attention toward a blue notebook that the other guide, Becky, holds in her hands.

"What is a journal?" Becky asks.

"Something you write down personal things in," a student responds.

"That's right! Great! Anyone else?" She beckons to the students, encouraging them with her eyes and gesturing for them to participate.

"It's something you write in to keep track of things, like the weather," another student adds.

"Wonderful." Becky nods approval to the student.

"It's like a diary," another student offers quickly.

"That's right. My, how many knowledgeable students we have here today." Becky smiles to each of the students in the group.

"The journal you will get for the Rite of Passage Experience is yours to keep. It is a record of your participation in the Rite of Passage Experience—ROPE. It contains stories for you to read. It has places for you to write or draw pictures about ROPE."

Stan hands the blue journals out to the students, who handle them excitedly, leafing through the pages.

Becky continues, "I'd like you to open to the page marked 'Session 1,' right at the beginning."

She waits as the students flip to the correct page. Holding a copy of the journal opened to the page marked "Session 1," she gives the students a point of reference.

"The page should look like this." She points to the page

titled "Session 1." On the center of the page there is a large circle cut into quarters. Beneath it, several questions are printed on the yellow paper, in black ink.   .

"Please take a moment to read and follow the instructions on the page." Becky reads the instructions aloud. "Write a word or draw a picture in each of the four pieces of the pie that describes how you feel right now. Then write a sentence using at least one of these four words to help explain this feeling. We will ask you to share what you have written, which you may do if you like."

Both Becky and Stan walk around the students, who hunch silently over their journals. Some students are thinking, eyes raised to the ceiling, pencils in mouths. Some are already writing.

Stan kneels next to a student, puts his hand on the student's shoulder, and asks, "How are you doing? Do you understand what we have asked you to do?"

The student gazes up at Stan, whose six-foot-two, 225-pound muscular frame dwarfs her. The student nods slowly. Almost inaudibly, she murmurs, "Yeah." Her eyes return to the journal. She slowly begins to write. Stan moves on to the next student.

"As with all the other exercises in the journal," Stan announces while the students finish writing, "we will tell you if we are going to see them or not. We may collect some things we ask you to write. We will tell you before we do this. Everything we collect we will return to you. We are not going to collect what you're writing now."

Stan and Becky look around the group, checking for the students to finish their assignment. One by one, heads look up, signaling completion.

"Would anyone like to share what they have written?" Becky asks. The students stare at a point in the middle of the circle. No one moves.

"I feel excited," Becky offers.

Stan follows by saying, "I feel a little nervous. I don't know any of you, so I wonder who you all are."

"I feel happy," John blurts out. "Happy we aren't in class," he adds. Everyone laughs.

"I feel nervous," Amanda says hesitantly, looking at Stan,

who smiles with understanding. More students contribute, until almost all have shared something.

"What do you think we need to know about each other before we go any farther?" Becky asks with a twinkle in her eye. The students stare back, mystified.

Stan picks up Becky's lead.

"You all know this about each other."

A moment of silence.

"We don't know your names?" David says.

"That's right," Becky responds.

The First Challenge

"Since you have all been together for some time, perhaps since kindergarten, we're sure you know each other's names by now," Becky continues. "We have a fun way to learn and remember each other's names. It's kind of challenging. Do you all know what a challenge is?"

"Something difficult," Charles responds.

"Yes, that is correct," Stan replies. "Does anyone else know what a challenge may mean?"

"An adventure, something daring," Mary adds.

"Something you have to work hard at," Joe suggests.

Becky sums up the students' responses. "That's right. All of you knew that a challenge was something difficult, which you work very hard to accomplish. Now, are you all ready to accept a challenge?"

"Yeah!" The students respond with excitement, nodding their heads as they lean forward in their chairs.

"Okay. Here is what we are going to do."

Becky points to Amanda, sitting at her immediate left, and says, "You will say your name. What is your name?"

The student replies, "Amanda."

"Fine. Now, Amanda says her name, and a favorite food that begins with the first letter of her name."

Becky puts her hand on Amanda's shoulder.

"What is a favorite food of yours that begins with the letter A, Amanda?"

Amanda smiles nervously and pauses, her eyes searching the ceiling for an answer. She slowly says, "Apples."

"Great!" Stan says.

"Now, the student sitting on the other side of Amanda repeats Amanda's name and her food, and then says his name and a favorite food that begins with the first letter of his name. This continues around the circle until everyone has a turn. Does everybody understand what the challenge is?"

Becky looks around the group of students. They nod.

A Teachable Moment

"What do you think we will need to do to accomplish this challenge?" Stan asks.

"We'll need to listen," Mary offers.

"That's right," Stan replies with a big smile. "What else?"

"Pay attention and think," Jennifer announces.

"Good!" exclaims Becky. "Let's see how well we can accomplish this challenge. Who do you think has the hardest part of this challenge?" Becky asks, with a worried look.

"You do," several of the students respond.

"Why?" Becky says.

"Because you are last and will have to remember what each of us has said," David says.

"Whew! That's right, David. I'm going to have to try real hard," Becky says.

"Okay, is everyone ready to begin? Do we all know what we need to do?" The students nod, silently signaling their readiness.

"Amanda, please start this challenge," Becky says.

"Amanda. Apples," she begins, with a little more certainty than before.

"Amanda, apples. Mary, muffins," Mary says excitedly, looking to Jennifer at her left.

"Amanda, apples. Mary, muffins." Jennifer pauses, glancing around the circle as some students giggle nervously. "Jennifer, jelly," she blurts out, pleased and relieved at her response.

Lisa, seated next to Jennifer, stares at the floor. The group is quiet.

John's voice breaks the silence. "Did you forget your name?"

Lisa looks up. "No!" she shoots back, staring at John. She grimaces, and then she looks over at Amanda.

"Amanda . . ." Another pause. She glances at Stan. Stan silently mouths the word "apple" to Lisa. With a quick smile, Lisa continues.

"Amanda, apples; Mary, muffins; Jennifer, jelly; Lisa . . ." Another pause as she looks at John with a "Nah, nah, nah, I know my name, you jerk!" look in her eyes: "Lasagna." Her eyes sparkle as everyone goes "Mmm," signaling approval of her choice.

The group members all perform the task with varying degrees of success.

"Charles, chips. Joe, jelly beans. John, junk food. David, doughnuts. And I'm Becky, and I like banana cream pie. All right, we did it! That was wonderful, everybody," Becky says encouragingly, and she begins to applaud. The group eagerly follows, clapping and smiling proudly.

"What did you need to do to accomplish this challenge of remembering everyone's name and a favorite food?" Stan asks.

"We had to listen and remember," Mary says.

Amy adds, "We had to pay attention."

"We needed to try real hard," Jennifer offers.

"We had to think and not fool around," Ellen states, looking at John with disapproval.

"That's right," Stan affirms, nodding. Making eye contact with all the students, he says slowly, "Throughout ROPE, we will be doing challenges that get more and more difficult. Did you think you could accomplish this challenge?"

Several of the students shake their heads no.

Stan continues, "You got a little tip about what you'll need to do to accomplish more difficult"—he pauses and looks around the group, allowing the drama to build—"*much* more difficult challenges."

The Group Sets Guidelines

"What kinds of things do you think we would need to think about in order to participate in and accomplish more difficult challenges?" Stan asks. He pauses as Becky gets up and walks to the sheet of newsprint on the easel behind her chair.

The students sit silently.

"We'd have to do all those things we said before, only do them harder?" Mary offers, shrugging.

"Yes, we'd all certainly have to try harder and do all those things you said before. Listen, pay attention, not fool around, think, and many other things," Stan adds.

Becky, now standing at the easel, continues.

"What guidelines will help us? How do we need to act in order to accomplish difficult and somewhat dangerous challenges?"

"Dangerous!" John blurts out.

The students sit wide-eyed.

"We'd have to be safe and careful if we were going to do anything dangerous," Charles says slowly.

"That is correct," Becky responds. "We would have to be careful and make sure everyone was safe." She writes "1. *SAFETY*" on the newsprint.

"Safety is the most important rule or guideline that we must follow. If we feel that someone is not safe, we may have to stop that person from continuing to participate in a particular challenge. This is one of the only times that Stan or I will actually stop you from doing something. What do you think rules are for?" Becky continues.

"To help you know what to do and how to act," Charles states with assurance.

"What would happen if there were no rules, laws, and regulations?" Stan asks.

"It would be great!" John quickly replies.

Only Joe laughs.

"It would be chaotic and dangerous," Mary says.

"That's probably true," Becky replies. "We only have to think of what driving would be like without rules to get a picture of how chaotic and dangerous it would be. I ask you all," she continues, "what would be useful for this group to think about for *our* rules?"

Stan reworks the same question. "What other guidelines do

you think we should have for this group in order to accomplish challenges together?"

"We should try things," Mary says.

"Great!" Becky writes, "2. *TRY IT*" on the newsprint. She emphasizes this point. "How can we accomplish anything if we don't try it?"

"What else?" Stan asks.

"We should try to listen to each other's ideas about things," David suggests.

"What do you mean?" Stan asks.

"Like if we're doing something, and somebody has an idea for how to accomplish a challenge, we should at least listen to that person."

"What is a word to describe what David has so nicely stated?" Becky asks.

The group stares at Becky.

"It's an important word . . . it starts with the letter r."

She writes the letter on the newsprint.

"*Respect*," Frank shouts out.

"That's right, Frank. *Respect*." Becky quickly completes the word she started on the newsprint: "3. *RESPECT*."

"These are wonderful rules that you have all come up with," she says. "I'm certain they will help this group accomplish many difficult challenges. There is just one more rule that Stan and I would like you to have. And that is"—Becky writes, "4. *SILENCE*."

"Do not tell any other students what you are doing in your ROPE group. Do you know why?" Becky asks.

"So we don't ruin it for other students who haven't done the stuff yet," Frank replies.

"Yes, that's part of it, Frank," she says encouragingly. "Also, we would like all students to experience each of the challenges without any prior information, so they won't know what to expect. In this way, it will be like everyday living. Since we are faced with new and different challenges almost every day, we'd like to offer you new and exciting challenges from which you will learn some important things."

Stan continues, "If you share any information about what

you did, other students may not get the most from their experience, and some people may get the wrong information."

"You can talk to your parents and teachers about what you do in ROPE," Becky says, "even older brothers and sisters, who may have done some of these things before. Okay? Can everyone follow and respect these rules? Can we all agree that they are important and will help us accomplish our challenges during ROPE?"

Some of the students in the group nod their heads, while others agree verbally. Stan and Becky ask each group member for commitment to following the rules. Everyone agrees to do so.

"We would like to welcome you to the first session of ROPE. Have any of you heard about ROPE before?" Becky asks.

Several of the students raise their hands.

Mary says, "My sister was in it, and she said it was fun."

"I heard that you climb some big mountain. Is that true?" Joe asks.

"Well," Becky begins, "I'm not sure what we will all be doing. But it will be special, and I know it will be fun."

Becky begins to write the word *FUN* on the newsprint under the list of rules.

"In fact, let's just make rule number one *FUN* to show it's an important thing," Becky adds, to the delight of the students. "What else have you heard?" she continues.

"I heard that we learn a lot of important things that help us when we get to junior high school," Ellen replies.

Several other students offer ideas and information about ROPE. Some information is fairly accurate. Other information has been distorted to mythical proportions.

"I am really impressed with how much you know about ROPE and am glad that you are enthusiastic and aware of the importance of ROPE," Stan says.

Becky says, "I'd like to know if anyone knows what ROPE stands for."

Several students look at their journal covers, which have "ROPE—Rite of Passage Experience" on the cover.

"Rite of Passage Experience!" David and Mary shout out together.

Becky asks, "How do you spell that?"

"*W-r-i-t-e,*" Jennifer offers.

"That's one way to spell it. What other ways can we spell the first word? What does this word mean?" Becky points to the word *WRITE* on the newsprint.

Ellen fumbles around for a better description. "It means to write something . . . you know, like with a pen or pencil on paper."

"Who knows where we can find the meanings of words?" Stan asks.

"In a dictionary!" several of the students respond at once.

"That's *right,*" Becky says, accenting the word. "And we happen to have one *right* over here." She points to Stan, who reaches under his chair to pick up a dictionary.

Holding it up, he asks, "Who can look up the word for us?"

John races up and seizes the book from Stan's hands. He sits back down and rustles through the pages.

"Write . . . to form or inscribe," he reads.

"Very good, John," Stan says. "How else can we spell the word?"

The students offer a variety of ways: *right, wright,* and *rite* are all looked up in the dictionary. Becky puts the definitions on the newsprint. This process continues for each of the words in the Rite of Passage Experience.

RITE — A ceremony with rules.

PASSAGE — Movement from one place to the next.

EXPERIENCE — Personal involvement in an event.

When the definitions are combined, a description of the Rite of Passage Experience emerges.

A ceremony to mark the change from one point in life to the next

Going from one place to the next

A ceremony that you participate in

Something you do that signifies a change

Learning about how to be an adult

Going from childhood to adulthood

Setting a Context for ROPE

A discussion ensues about the purpose of rituals of initiation and about why the students are participating in a modern-day rite of passage.

"Your principal and your teachers feel that you are very special and important people," Becky begins. "Because of this, and because they care about you very much, they wanted you to have this special and important experience. We believe, along with your principal and your teachers, that you are special and that at this point in your education you are in a unique situation because of what you will be doing next year. This is different from what you have done in the years before. Can anyone tell me what will be different for you next year?"

Becky looks around the group, waiting for a response. Several students glance at one another thoughtfully.

Mary offers slowly, "We'll be going into a different school?"

"That's right!" Stan responds.

"As you know," Becky continues, "this is a special time, not only because you are leaving elementary school but also because you are changing and entering a period of your life that is somewhat different from anything you have experienced before. Does anyone know what this special period of your life is called?"

Again, Becky scans the group for a response. This time, the students exchange smiles and snickers. Whispering, interspersed with outbursts of laughter, can be heard.

"Puberty," Frank blurts out. His cheeks redden.

"That's right!" Stan responds. "And what are you called at this period of your life?"

"Teenager," Mary calls out.

"Teenager," David quickly follows.

"That's good," Becky begins. "Most of you have indicated that you are entering a period known as puberty or adolescence or being a teenager. Because of this, we would like to explore some of the things that teenagers have to do to be happy, and also some of the important skills that they must have in order to do well in junior high school next year and as adults in the future." Becky pauses, making eye contact and nodding support to each of the students.

"How old are you?" Becky continues.

"Eleven," Amanda says.

"Twelve," John replies.

"So most of you are between the ages of eleven and twelve. Maybe some of you are ten. How old will some of you be in a year?" Becky asks.

"Thirteen," Charles replies.

"Is there anything different about being thirteen, compared to being eleven or twelve?" Stan asks, accentuating *teen*.

"You're a teenager? A teen?" Amy offers.

"That's right!" Stan responds, with a big smile. "You are teenagers. One of the things we want to explore is what it means to be a teenager. What do you think being a teenager means?"

"Being a teenager means you have more responsibilities," Mary says assertively.

"Being a teen means you have sex!" John quips, with an explosion of embarrassed laughter from the group.

"Well, okay," Becky responds slowly, but with no show of support or agreement. "What else?"

"We have to make important decisions," Frank offers.

Stan follows up, looking at Frank. "Yes. What kinds of decisions, Frank?"

Frank shrugs his shoulders, casting knowing glances to select group members. "Like whether to drink or do drugs. What courses to take in school. Things like that."

"Good. That's right," Stan says approvingly.

The group offers a number of examples of decisions to be made in the future. Together, the students go on exploring what it means to be a teenager.

Becky continues her presentation, to set the stage and provide a context for the Rite of Passage Experience. She guides the students toward greater understanding of the historical context of rituals of initiation. Her gentle, knowing voice holds the students' attention.

"There are many different kinds of people who belong to groups known as cultures and societies. Within every culture, there are different ways in which people know when they become adults.

In some cultures, several hundred years ago, we know young people went through a clear and uniform experience in order to become adults. Cultures had rituals and ceremonies for their children, to give them the status of adults. Remember, last night we saw a videotape about different cultural rituals of initiation."

Becky pauses and looks around the group. The students nod silently.

"We saw that different cultures do special things with their young people, so that the young people will function and be looked upon by the rest of the culture as adults. Can you give me an example of a ceremony or ritual today that young people go through on their passage from childhood to adulthood?"

"Confirmation," Mary offers.

"Yes." Stan motions to the rest of the group. "Anyone else?"

"Bar mitzvah," Amy says quietly.

"Great, Amy. That is correct," Becky says. "Even today, some cultures in other parts of the world have rites of passage. A long time ago on our continent, people also had rituals and ceremonies in which a young person participated to become an adult. For example, the Native Americans had a ceremony where a young person typically had to go out in the woods and take care of himself for several days by hunting, preparing a shelter, and feeding himself. In preparation for this, he would go off with certain village elders, teachers who would guide him in the ways of the world. After completing this challenge in the woods, he returned to his village but was not able to return to his parents' home. Instead, he was provided with a shelter where all his belongings were placed. From that time on, he was viewed by family, friends, and the community or culture as an adult. He was responsible for all the tasks that an adult would perform and had a clear understanding of his role in the adult society. How would you know when someone is an adult in society today?"

"When you graduate from high school," Mary says.

"When you can buy alcohol," John adds.

"When you get your driver's license," Jennifer offers.

"When you have babies," John says.

"When you get a job," Charles says.

Becky is writing all the responses on the newsprint. "What

are some other ways you know someone is an adult in the world today?''

"When you move out of your parents' house," Ellen responds.

"When you pay taxes," David adds.

"When you get married," Amanda states.

Becky finishes writing on the newsprint.

"I bet we could probably think of a few more if we had the time. How old are you when you graduate from high school?" Becky asks, pointing to "high school" on the newsprint.

"Seventeen or eighteen," Charles replies.

"Okay. How old are you when you can buy alcohol?" Becky continues down the list, writing responses as she goes.

"Twenty-one, legally," John responds, smiling.

"How about driving and working?" Becky continues.

"Sixteen and fifteen," several students respond.

"So we see that there is no particular age or thing you do which means you are an adult." Becky pauses to make eye contact with each of the students. "Together with your principal and teachers, we know that there are important skills and knowledge which you must know in order to be a happy and successful adult. There are important skills and knowledge which you will need to know in order to successfully go on your journey or passage to adulthood. What we are going to do here in **ROPE** is give you opportunities to learn these important skills and knowledge, so you will have an easier time on your passage from childhood to adulthood. Our experience will be different. It will include a series of physical and thinking challenges that you will need to attempt to accomplish, both as individuals and as a group. We will help you learn skills and those things which you will need to know in order to be adults in our town and society."

Becky pauses, looking intently at each student.

"Skills you will need to survive the passage from child to adult. Does anyone remember what we said a challenge is?" Becky asks.

"Something difficult that you do," Charles responds.

"Yes. As we said, you are going to be challenged to accomplish important tasks, so you will learn many lifesaving skills. Are we ready to try a challenge?''

The students respond eagerly and begin to stand.

A Teachable Moment Is Created

Stan motions the group to where he has already positioned himself. "Please form a circle over here."

Becky, holding a thirty-foot length of one-inch-thick purple-striped rope, joins the group.

"Has anyone heard of the *Titanic*?" she asks, with a mischievous twinkle in her eye.

"Yeah, that's the boat that hit an iceberg and sank, right?" Frank says.

"That is correct," Becky replies. "Let's pretend we're all passengers on the *Titanic*."

"Oh, no!" John shrieks. "Let's get to a lifeboat!" He continues to yell with excitement as several of the students begin to laugh.

"You are right, John," Stan says quickly. John looks bewildered, expecting to be reprimanded for his outburst. "And, as you see, Becky is placing the rope in a circle on the floor."

Stan points to the rope, which Becky has arranged on the floor in a circle of about fifteen feet in diameter.

"Here is your life raft," Becky says. She looks at each of the students. "In order for you to survive, everyone must fit on this life raft."

"Do you think you can get everyone on this life raft?" Stan asks.

The students nod, and several begin getting into the circle. Others follow. Some sit on the floor.

"All right! It looks as if everyone easily got on the life raft. Now, please get off," Stan orders.

Dutifully, all the students return to the outside of the circle.

"There is one interesting thing about this life raft," Becky begins, as she bends down to adjust the size of the circle. She makes it smaller, about ten feet in diameter. "It has a leak in it. As you can see, it is gradually getting smaller. Now let's see how we can all fit on the life raft. I think I can see a rescue ship approaching on the horizon."

Becky pretends to look into the distance, her hand over her eyes as if blocking the sun.

The students, effortlessly and without discussion, again "board" the life raft.

"All right. Once again, you have accomplished this part of the challenge. Great!" Stan says. "Now, please disembark from your life raft. Your rescue ship is steaming closer. I think it will be here soon."

Becky again adjusts the rope circle, making it smaller, about five feet in diameter. The raft continues to get smaller, and the students enthusiastically attempt each challenge. As the raft diminishes in size and the challenge becomes more difficult, the students engage in lively discussion about how to accomplish the challenge.

"I bet if we try real hard, we can get on an even smaller raft," Becky says.

"Oh, no!" several of the students moan as Becky begins reducing the size of the raft to about three feet in diameter. Immediately, the students begin sharing ideas about how to accomplish the challenge. After only a few moments, they employ a modified version of their last effort and accomplish the challenge.

"You've done it again!" Becky shouts with delight.

The students, clinging together to remain on the raft, lose their balance and stumble to standing positions around the small raft. Their cheers and applause fill the room.

"Would you all please take a seat right here on the floor around your raft? Your rescue ship has arrived. Congratulations! You have survived and are rescued. I think you have done so well that you deserve to give yourselves another round of applause."

Becky's applause is quickly followed by that of all the students, who cheer wildly.

Stan commends the students. "What a wonderful effort!"

"Yes, indeed!" Becky adds. "The first time, when the raft was large, what did you need to do to get everyone on it?"

Mary shrugs. "We didn't need to do anything special, just get on."

"How about the last few times? What did you need to do to get everyone on the raft?" Becky asks.

"We had to talk and make a plan," David answers.

"Yes. What else?"

"We had to cooperate and work together," Amanda says.

"We had to trust each other," Ellen responds.

"We had to work real hard," Joe offers.

"That is right," Becky says. "It is important to know that all the challenges in ROPE will be more and more difficult. You will need to remember what you did to accomplish this challenge, in order for you to be as successful at accomplishing the next challenges."

Becky pauses to allow the group to think.

Stan asks, "Did you think you could get everyone on the raft the last time?"

"No way," John replies, shaking his head.

"I'll bet many of you thought that you would not be able to accomplish the challenge. I am impressed that you all tried as hard as you did. It is important to remember that you can never accomplish what you don't try," Stan states, again allowing the message to sink in.

"What roles did people play during the final challenge?" Becky asks.

The students look confused.

Becky rephrases the question. "What roles do people play on a ship?"

"Captain, crew . . . ," Charles responds and is quickly cut off by John, who says, "Passengers and cooks."

"That's right," Becky says. "Who was a captain on the raft? Who was being a leader?"

The students discuss the different roles they all played during the challenge. They identify themselves as leaders, helpers, followers, and observers. They discuss how each of these roles is important to the group's success.

"Many of you played a number of different roles in a very short period of time," Becky says. "Today you completed the first of the thirteen meetings that you will have during this phase of your Rite of Passage Experience. Together, we learned each other's names. We set up some important guidelines to follow, so we can accomplish many challenges."

Becky points to the list of guidelines on the newsprint. "We learned more about why you are all on a rite of passage and participating in ROPE—because you are all entering an important period of your life, known as adolescence, which is the transition, the passage, between childhood and adulthood."

Becky pauses, and the students sit attentively.

"We had an opportunity to attempt and in fact accomplish a difficult challenge," she continues. "You learned what you must do in order to accomplish difficult challenges—work together, cooperate, and help and trust each other. It's important to make a plan and listen to everyone's ideas, if you are going to accomplish even more difficult challenges in the future."

"Please open your journals to the first story, 'The Journey,' " Stan says. "This is a very interesting story. To prepare for our next session, please read and answer the questions that follow the story. It was wonderful to meet all of you. Becky and I look forward to seeing you in two days and, over the next six weeks, helping you on your Rite of Passage Experience."

Stan dismisses the students, who are accompanied back to their classroom.

Twice a week during the next six weeks, the groups engage in a series of activities and challenges that help them learn important skills and knowledge. These include problem solving and decision making, how to work cooperatively in a group, and understanding the impact of peer pressure on decision making while learning to believe in oneself and one's capabilities—ultimately, learning to trust oneself and others.

7

The Culminating Challenge

The first phase of the Rite of Passage Experience culminates in an adventure. It could be rock climbing and rappelling, a long hike, an orienteering course, a solo in the woods, a ropes course, an overnight camping trip, mountain climbing, or any other event that allows students to utilize all the skills they have learned in the previous ROPE sessions.

So far, the group we have been describing in the previous chapter has participated in eleven sessions over roughly sixteen hours. The students have engaged in a variety of challenges designed to produce a "teachable moment." They have been preparing for their culminating challenge.

Stan and Becky, the two ROPE guides, appear at the classroom door. The students are abuzz with excitement.

"May we have the Ropers up here by the door?" Becky requests.

Eleven students rise quickly in response to Becky's call. The Ropers, a name these students selected for themselves during the fourth session, clutch brown-bag lunches, knapsacks, hats, coats, and their courage as they head out of the classroom.

They walk quietly down the hall, toward the front doors of the school. Greeting them as they pass through the doors are three more community elders, two parents, and a teacher. Together, they walk toward the bus that is waiting for them. The principal stands in the doorway waving goodbye and wishing them luck.

Once everyone is seated, Stan begins.

"Let us get our contracts out and review our individual and group goals. Does everyone have the contract that we worked on the other day?"

The students look at one another, nodding yes as they search for the sheets of paper on which their contracts are written.

"What would you like to accomplish today? What is your individual goal? Anyone?"

Stan looks at the students, waiting for a response.

"My goal for today is to try to climb and rappell," Mary reads from her contract.

"Great!" Stan responds. "And what would you like the group to do to help you accomplish your goal?"

"I would like the group to encourage me by telling me I can do it."

"Will you help Mary accomplish her goal?" Stan asks the group.

"Yes," several students respond at once. All heads nod.

"Who else will now share his or her goal with the group?" Stan continues. "Remember, we must all know what the others are trying to accomplish and how we can help."

"I'm going to try not to fool around so much," John offers, with unusual seriousness. The students look surprised. Some exchange doubtful glances.

"That is a fine goal, John. How would you like the group to help you accomplish this challenging goal?" Stan asks.

"I would like the group to help me accomplish my goal by not egging me on, and by reminding me what my goal is if I start to fool around," John responds.

Lisa, usually shy, thrusts her hand up, wishing to present her goal next. Stan nods at Lisa, who begins.

"I will attempt to be brave and try all the challenges. I will also help others," she announces.

Stan encourages her, pleased that Lisa acknowledges her timidity in her goal to be brave. "That is a wonderful goal, Lisa."

One by one, the students report their personal goals. "To try all the challenges," one student offers. Several more students talk about trusting others, working together to help everyone accomplish goals, not fooling around, and following directions and being safe.

"You have all chosen very challenging goals. Goals that are worthy of good efforts. Goals that will require all of you to help each other. When you accomplish your personal goals, how do you think you will feel?" Stan asks.

"We'll feel good!" John exclaims.

"We'll feel proud of ourselves," Amy adds.

"If we all accomplish our goals, we'll feel like we can do anything," Mary says.

"What does this group want to set as the group goal?" Becky asks.

The students look at their contracts. Several hands go up. Charles is recognized and begins.

"The Ropers have as their group goal to help each other accomplish the challenges and to make decisions about how to successfully and safely rock climb and rappell," he says, to the approval of the rest of the students.

"Well put, Charles," Mary offers, somewhat mockingly. Soft giggles are heard throughout the bus.

"We want to help each other through these challenges by remembering what we learned in ROPE," Frank says, looking at his contract.

"Yes," Stan responds. "And if you accomplish all your goals, not only will you feel great, you will have fun, too. Remember, your efforts and attempts are all we can ask for. Being here on the bus, ready to go, proves you are already trying. Are you ready to attempt a challenge?"

The students respond with excitement: "Yeah!" The bus slowly departs. Young children peer out of classroom windows and wave goodbye. The journey from childhood continues.

The bus ride is relatively quiet, as student bus rides go. Within twenty-five minutes, the bus is weaving along a hilly country road. The bus manuevers around another sharp curve, and there it is.

"Is that the cliff?" Mary shrieks.

"Oh, my!" Amy blurts out.

Stan beckons out the front windshield, toward the cliff appearing around the curve, about a quarter of a mile in the distance. "There she be."

The chatter of anticipation begins to fill the bus. The students all stare at the cliff, craning their necks, their faces pressed against the bus windows. The squeal of the brakes sends a shiver through the students as the bus pulls off the road and onto a thin shoulder in front of a dirt road leading up to the cliff. Several more adult guides, who have been preparing at the cliff for over an hour, greet the students as they arrive. The students and the adults exit the bus and stand in the shadow of the cliff, which rises several hundred feet above the road.

"Let's stand over here in a circle," Becky says as she positions herself at the foot of the dirt road.

Nicki, a well-outfitted climbing expert and four-foot-eleven dynamo of enthusiasm, helps move the students and adults toward the circle. She hands out the helmets as she greets the students and the adults with a smile and a firm handshake.

"Here is a helmet," Nicki says. "Please try it on. We can help you adjust the straps to make it fit snugly."

A loose circle begins to take shape. Twelve students and seven adults fidget with helmet straps. Knapsacks, brown-bag lunches, articles of clothing, and anxious excitement surround the group.

"We will be wearing these helmets at all times unless instructed otherwise by one of the guides," Becky announces as the group focuses its attention on her. "To begin, it would be helpful if we all knew each other's names. Nicki and Don"—Becky points to the two adults who greeted the group—"are here to help us today. Why don't we all introduce ourselves?"

Immediately, John says, "I'm John, and I like junk food!"

The group shifts anxiously, recalling John's goal of not fooling around. Quickly sensing the dilemma, Becky refocuses John's pronouncement in a positive way.

"That's a neat idea, John," she says. "Let's do the name

game. Who can tell those who have not done this before how it works?''

The group breathes a sigh of relief as Mary tells the group how the name game was performed in the first session.

''. . . And then Becky repeats everyone's name and her favorite food, beginning with the first letter of her name.'' Mary smiles mischievously and looks at Becky, who rolls her eyes skyward.

The introductions go quickly. At Becky's request, the students review their group and individual goals and the guidelines the group has agreed to follow during the first session.

''Respect all members of the group,'' Amanda says.

''Try all challenges,'' Frank says.

''Be safe,'' Jennifer says.

''And have fun!'' David offers, completing the review of the group guidelines.

Becky points over her shoulder. ''We now seem ready to walk down this road over here. Is everyone ready? Are your helmets on snug and secure?''

The group members nod or say yes.

''Be careful, and watch your step,'' Stan advises.

They silently set off on the mile-long hike to the bottom of the cliff.

Fifteen minutes later, the group collects itself at the foot of a steep rocky path of about a forty-five-degree angle, which leads to the bottom of the climbing and rappelling site. Everyone stands in silence. All eyes stare up at the sheer cliff at the end of the rocky path. There are anxious sighs and expressions of fear as the students move gingerly over the boulders on the path that brings them to the bottom of the cliff.

Once again, the group collects itself at the base of the cliff, about seventy-five yards above the path. Standing cautiously on a five-foot-narrow path, Becky points to several multicolored ropes hanging down the side of the rock face.

''This is climb number one,'' Becky says, holding a rope right in front of her. ''Over there is the rappel.'' She points. ''And down there is climb number two.''

The students stand in silence and gaze at the ropes. Their

heads move up and down as they survey the climbing and rappelling site.

"I can't believe this," one of the students mumbles.

"We're really going to do this?" another adds in a disbelieving tone.

"We are all going to go up this path to the top of the cliff." Becky points to a narrow gully winding around the side of the cliff. "It is very steep. We have these rope handrails to help you up. Go up slowly, one at a time, please."

Becky leads the way. One by one, the students ascend the cliff.

At the top, they gather again in a circle. They put on safety harnesses and receive a lesson on the belay system. This gives students hands-on experience with the safety system. One by one, students fasten themselves to a rope with a carabiner. The rope is held in the belay position by another student perched at the top of the ten-foot precipice, next to a climbing staff. Don speaks gently to Amy.

"With your left hand, hold the rope that comes up from the climber against your right thigh. You hold the rope firmly with your left hand and let the rest of the rope pass through your right hand, positioned at your right hip. There—see how the rope goes nicely around your back?" Don says, as Amy easily follows his directions.

Fifteen feet below, Stan helps John clip onto the other end of the rope that Amy is holding.

"Now, John, after you are fastened onto this rope that Amy's holding, you'll need to communicate to her. When you are at the bottom of the cliff, the person who is belaying you at the top will not be able to see you. You will have to communicate clearly, so you can work safely together. Here is the way you can do this."

Stan instructs John in the same communication system that Don teaches Amy.

"After you are clipped in and an adult checks the lock on the carabiner, to make sure it is properly closed, you call out loud to your belayer: ON BELAY?"

Stan loudly pronounces the phrase, which startles John and echoes through the hills.

"This means that you are prepared and secured to the belay

system and ready to climb. It asks the belayer if he or she is ready and asks another person to accept responsibility for you, for your safety."

"After the climber says, 'On belay,'" Don says to Amy, "and if you are prepared to accept the responsibility for someone else's safety, you say, 'BELAY ON.' This is your contract with the other person. It means he or she can trust you to help accomplish a difficult challenge safely."

Don's firm tone is impressive on this important point. Amy looks wide-eyed at Don and then toward John on the other end of her rope.

"BELAY ON!" Amy yells to John.

"If the rope is not tight between you and your belayer, call, 'UP ROPE!'" Again Stan calls loudly, looking up at Amy: "UP ROPE!"

Amy begins to slide the rope through her left hand and around her back, through her right hand.

"Don't ever let your right hand leave the rope, not even for a second," Don tells Amy.

The rope moves up the rocky incline, toward Amy.

Stan says, "When the rope is tight, yell 'That's me.'"

John watches as the rope begins to tighten.

"THAT'S ME!" John yells to Amy as the rope lifts off the rock and becomes a tight bond between John and Amy.

"Before you climb, you must ask permission from the belayer. CLIMBING?" Stan yells up to Amy. "This is your way of asking permission to climb. If your belayer gives permission, she yells back."

Stan looks up at Amy, who has already been coached by Don.

"CLIMB ON!" Amy yells to John.

John begins to walk carefully up the rock incline. Amy dutifully moves the rope between her hands.

Midway up the practice climb, Stan says, "John, I want you to stop right there. Make sure there is tension on the rope. Now, lean back. Let all your weight hang on the rope."

John begins to lean back. The rope strains tighter. Amy smiles at John as he puts all his weight on the rope. He is completely in her hands. Amy smiles with delight at her ability to hold John safely.

"Wow! This is neat!" John says, completely dependent on Amy.

"Okay. Now you can finish the climb. I just wanted both of you to see how the system works," Stan says.

John quickly climbs the next seven feet. Don motions to John to sit next to Amy, and John immediately complies.

"Now, Amy's job is not complete until you are seated beside her and you say, 'Off belay!'" Don says to John.

John quickly replies, "Off belay!"

"Now, Amy, to end your contract with John, you say, 'Belay off.'"

"Belay off," Amy responds, looking at John.

"Thanks! You saved my life!" John says, playfully patting Amy on the shoulder. Her smile stretches from ear to ear.

This scenario is repeated over the next hour, with two practice climbs going on simultaneously. Each student practices the roles of climber and belayer. All the students are eager to try. They watch one another carefully, helping one another remember the communications and how to climb and belay safely.

By half past eleven, all practice has been completed. The students gather for a quick lunch and a final group discussion about the challenge ahead. Spontaneously, they sit close in a circle.

"This is an important day in all of your lives," Becky begins in a solemn tone. "Seven weeks ago, we first met all of you. You were children beginning your Rite of Passage Experience. Today, you have an opportunity to use all you have learned and apply it to a most difficult challenge. What have you learned that would be helpful to you during this challenge?"

"I learned that if I try real hard, I can do more than I think I can do," Lisa responds.

"When I'm on a difficult part of the climb or rappel and I'm feeling kind of scared, I can use the part of problem solving that tells me to calm down, so I can solve the problem," David says, finishing a doughnut.

"I think I'll be able to trust whoever is going to belay me when I'm on a climb," Jennifer adds.

"We have all accomplished other difficult challenges during ROPE by helping and encouraging each other. I think that will really help us here today," Mary says with certainty.

"Yes. What each of you has said will certainly help you accomplish the challenges still before you," Becky replies. "How have you felt in the past when you have accomplished one of the difficult challenges?"

"Great!" Joe quickly responds. "Like when we found the markers in the woods with the compass, or got everyone on the small raft," he says with pride.

"Did you have fun?" Becky asks.

"Yeah!" several of the students eagerly call out.

"It was really fun when we did the trust falls," Frank offers.

"Remember when we talked before about having fun?" Becky says. Several of the students nod. "It is one of the most important challenges you will face when you get older. How are you going to have fun and feel good? Throughout ROPE, you all accomplished difficult challenges, which you felt good about and had fun doing. This is one of the most important things that you can remember. Having fun and feeling good can occur when you accomplish difficult challenges that you work hard for. Today, your good efforts will be rewarded by your feeling great about your accomplishments, and I'm sure you will all have fun."

The group finishes lunch just as Stan says, "Well, what do you think, Ropers? Are we ready to go for it?"

Several of the students jump up. "Yeah! Let's do it!"

Students and adults move quickly to designated locations. Excitement fills the air. Three adults slip into belay harnesses and move to the edge of the cliff.

"All right. Who is going to rappel first?" Becky asks from her position just behind the rappel location. The group stands behind the rope guard, talking excitedly and trying to decide who will go first.

"I'll go first!" Mary finally says boldly, half expecting someone to debate her for this honor.

No one objects. Mary looks somewhat surprised. It's too late. An adult takes her by the hand and leads her over the rope guard, toward the edge of the cliff. Becky quickly clips the belay rope to Mary.

Mary is breathing rapidly. "Oh, no! I can't believe I'm going to do this!"

"You'll do fine. You're on belay," Becky says in a very soothing tone. "Remember what David said before about calming down before you attempt to solve this problem."

With that, Becky positions herself at the edge of the cliff, her legs dangling. She is secured by a rope tied from her harness to a tree, some twenty yards away.

Mary creeps slowly backward toward the edge of the cliff. Still panting, she looks forward, toward the other students, who stare at her in silence. Amy watches, nervously biting the collar of her jacket.

"I can't believe it. I can't believe it. I can't do this," Mary says, and she lunges forward, away from the edge of the cliff, landing on her hands and knees.

Becky turns to look over her shoulder at Mary. "Okay. Let's think about what we are doing. Do you want to accomplish this difficult challenge?" she asks Mary softly.

"Yes," Mary responds, almost inaudibly.

"What do you have to do to accomplish this?"

"Try it. Give it a good effort," Mary responds, a little more loudly.

"Can you give it a good effort?" Becky asks.

Standing up and returning to the edge of the cliff, Mary takes a deep breath and says, "I'm ready now. On belay," she adds, almost as a reminder to herself.

"Yep, you're on belay," Becky acknowledges with a grin. "That's it. Just go very slowly. I've got you. Just remember to keep your butt out over the edge of the cliff first."

Slowly, Mary leans back over the edge of the cliff. Her eyes are open so wide that they look as if they may pop out of her head. She stares at Becky. Her hands shake as she lets the rope move through them.

"AAAHHHH!" Mary screams as she moves her foot off the top of the cliff and places it on the vertical rock face. Her other foot quickly follows. "I can't believe I'm doing this," she says again, with a small laugh. She continues moving down the rock face until only her head is visible above the edge of the cliff.

"How are you doing there?" Becky asks.

"Great! This is unbelievable!"

"Wave to everyone, Mary. Wave with your left hand," Becky says. "Your left hand is not really doing anything."

Becky waves to her. Mary returns the wave as the rest of the students wave back and yell, "Way to go, Mary. You're doing great." All the students start to cheer for Mary as she continues down.

Stan waits for her at the bottom. Mary's descent puts her right above Stan's head.

"Hello," Stan says as Mary lowers herself right next to him.

"That was awesome!" Mary screams as her feet touch the ground. All the students yell congratulatory remarks.

"Nice job," Stan says. "How do you feel about accomplishing this challenge?"

"I feel great!" Mary says. "Can I do it again?"

"You can try a climb in a minute," Stan tells her.

Several students gather around Mary, patting her on the back.

All the students accomplish at least one climb or rappel. Most accomplish both. The next two and a half hours go by quickly and are full of anxiety, excitement, joy, pride, and celebration of the group's accomplishments.

The announcement calling the group back to the bus is greeted with booing and regret. Students and adults move quickly to collect all the knapsacks, clothes, and equipment and head down the path toward the road. The walk back to the road is full of laughter and retold tales of individual accomplishment.

At the end of the path, just before the road at the edge of the woods, Becky asks the group to sit in a circle.

"What did you learn or discover about yourself or the group today?" she begins.

"I learned that we really can do more than we think we can if we try real hard," Lisa offers.

"I learned how to climb and rappell," Charles adds.

"I learned that we can trust each other a whole lot, and that people care about each other in this group," Jennifer says.

"I think we all accomplished a lot," John says seriously.

"I feel like we've been through a passage or something. Like it's different now. I don't know, I can't explain it," Frank says with some confusion.

The students talk for about fifteen minutes. They review their contracts and evaluate how they did at accomplishing their individual and group goals. Their pride is evident.

"You have all done terrific today. I know I speak for all your guides and the other adults when I tell you that we are very proud of you," Becky says slowly, looking into all the students' eyes. "Today marks another milestone on your Rite of Passage Experience. Many of you have found inner strength that you didn't know you had. Some gave their strength to others. You have all acted more like adults than like children. Remember how it feels to accomplish a difficult challenge. It feels great, and you have fun. That is one of the secrets of life."

Becky pauses again, looking at all the students. The moment is full of drama. The students spontaneously put their arms around one another's shoulders. For the moment, their transformation is evident even to them.

Becky challenges them one more time. "Do you think we can all stand up together with our arms around each other's shoulders?"

"We can do anything," Mary shouts.

"One, two, three—UP!" Becky orders.

Together, they rise effortlessly and cheer as the bus arrives to pick them up: one more challenge accomplished.

8

Transitions to Adulthood

The first phase of the Rite of Passage Experience is intended to lay a foundation of knowledge, in a developmentally and culturally relevant context, for students making the transition from childhood to adulthood. It provides opportunities to learn important attitudes, skills, beliefs, and values while engaging students and their families in a community process.

The process continues during the second and third phases of the strategy. It requires community development and coordination activities, which ensure that adequate and appropriate resources are available. This is no simple or easy task; it requires a significant commitment on the part of the community. Here is how it works.

Recall the Ropers, the student group discussed in previous chapters. After its culminating challenge (in this case, rock climbing and rappelling), the group met one more time. During the last meeting, the students reviewed the other sessions, identifying what they had accomplished and learned. Their guides continually linked the students' learning to later applications in their lives, pointing out that each time they had accomplished a difficult challenge, they felt great and had fun.

The Second Phase

The stage is set for the group's entry into the second phase of the Rite of Passage Experience. The students are challenged to select three different areas in which they would like to develop skills. Sports, computers, science, drama, and many others are discussed and selected from a community resource guide. The challenge is for them to learn how to accomplish something difficult, which they can feel good about and have fun doing.

At the last session, each student completes a contract, identifying which three positive leisure-time activities have been selected. The contract is signed by the student and the ROPE guides. It will also be mailed home for parents to sign. Parents are already prepared, through their participation in ROPE, to guide their children toward these positive activities during the next several years of school. The contracts are shared with junior high school guidance counselors, who will also help guide participation in the positive activities.

The primary parts of the students' world—family, school, and community—are linked to form a safety net. The link provides direction, which helps ensure safe passage for these children on their journey from childhood to adulthood.

Phase two is not just about making recreational activities available in the community. Two essential, dynamic ingredients of this phase must be underscored.

First, the community and the schools must collaborate to develop and make available a wide variety of interesting, enjoyable, productive opportunities for *all* school youth to engage in. Opportunities must continue to support positive development by promoting students' use of skills, as taught in the first phase of the modern-day rite of passage. There must be coaching and guidance, to ensure that each young person has some positive leisure-time activity to experiment with. These activities must be available after school and on weekends and must be geographically accessible to students.

Second, schools must work with parents and the community to identify and provide opportunities for parents and the community to participate in school-related enhancement activities. Harnessing the energies and creativity of parents and teachers supports and enhances children's connection to the community and their academic achievement.

Here again, it is important to keep in mind that the community has already made a commitment to providing and coordinating the resources necessary for successful implementation of the strategy. Communities that employ this or any other comprehensive primary prevention strategy have policymakers—administrators from education and government—who have all bought into the strategy and have responsibility for coordination of the necessary resources and services for the second and third phases. In keeping with the theoretical underpinnings of rituals of initiation, the community elders coordinate their efforts to transmit important prosocial values, beliefs, behaviors, and attitudes to youth.

The Third Phase

The third phase of this modern-day rite of passage begins in high school. It emerged from the idea that there are at least three identifiable, clear sets of beliefs and behaviors that we expect to see in adults. Neither is addressed systematically in a typical formal public education program.

First, we believe that helping others is a virtuous and desirable quality. Working together for the common good is a fundamental underpinning of a democratic society. Second, most young people grow up to become parents, and we hope that they will understand something about being good people and good parents. Third, whether we consider it or not, we all have a relationship with the earth, our environment. By and large, none of this is conveyed strategically in the schools. "Back to basics" does not provide an understanding of how to participate in a democracy, help others, be better parents, or become good stewards of the earth. Transmitting these important beliefs and behaviors is left to the family, to churches, or to chance. A critical element is missing from individuals' and the culture's experience. Young people and society benefit from specific experiences that transmit the culturally expected behaviors and beliefs of parenting, democracy, and giving to others.

During the third phase of the intervention, students are required to participate in community service. Once again, the ROPE guides from the first and second phases, along with parents, school personnel, and the community at large, assist students in their engagement with community service.

School curricula are expanded to include child and human

development courses. In the ideal situation, every high school student would have an opportunity to be in a child development and parenting course, with a laboratory experience of working in a day-care center. These high school students with special training could also assist with the implementation of the first phase of the Rite of Passage Experience as a community service project.

To experience giving and helping presents opportunities to feel and learn important human qualities. Compassion, sharing, cooperating, giving, and helping are not built on concrete, cognitively oriented instructional material or encouraged by slogans. Experiencing the feelings that result from human interactions that involve these important human qualities is critical for transmitting these important values and beliefs.

There are many opportunities in a community to provide valuable voluntary service for young people—to name just a few, there are scouting; care of the community's elderly, handicapped, infants, and toddlers; and assistance with the care and maintenance of public places, including school buildings and grounds. Environmental awareness projects are another way to explore the value of community service and responsible care for the planet earth. All these activities and involvements help youth feel connection, belonging, and being needed. Young people, previously segregated in schools, will become an integral, valuable part of their communities—which, in fact, they will soon inherit.

The Rite of Passage Experience is just one example of a primary prevention strategy that occurs for a whole community. As one parent stated, "ROPE provides something for parents and children to hang on to during the turbulent journey through adolescence. It give parents and children a language to share during this important time. It gives the community a vehicle to rally around while helping children cross the threshold from childhood to adulthood."

Certainly, there is no guarantee that the development of a modern-day rite of passage will cure all the symptoms plaguing our teenagers. Nevertheless, widespread historical evidence supports the use of formalized, culturally and ethnically relevant societal rituals during the passage from childhood to adulthood. In our rush to use technology, we overlook one of the primary and necessary psychosocial and cultural processes. We have not really considered how rites of passage have served as comprehensive primary prevention strategies. Again, I offer for your consideration: What would our culture be like without weddings, birthdays, or funerals? How many of us would get lost on our journey through life without these beacons to aid our navigation?

9

Key Ingredients
for Successful Intervention

It would be a significant consideration for those in the prevention business to understand and recognize the minimum conditions that must exist in a community before a primary prevention strategy has a chance of success. What follows is the identification of a series of essential ingredients that seem to be related to a community's readiness and ability to develop, implement, and sustain a comprehensive primary prevention strategy. It is no accident that I have focused significant attention on the composition and function of what I refer to as the *core group*. The ingredients necessary for a functioning core group concern the critical nature of collaboration and the process orientation of many working models of primary prevention. For a core group to be empowered in the service of developing and implementing a primary prevention strategy, minimum conditions must be present in the community. These minimum conditions set a context for the support and growth of a functioning core group, which is integral to the development and implementation of a primary prevention strategy.

Building Walls or Bridges?

Consider the ten minimum conditions required for implementing the Rite of Passage Experience for the group of students and their parents that we followed for part of a ROPE journey:

1. There was collaboration among school, community, and families and a commitment on their part to take primary prevention seriously. This is no minor point. Collaboration and commitment provide a firm foundation for the successful implementation of comprehensive primary prevention projects.

2. Teachers were involved in supporting the students through the Rite of Passage Experience and observed many of the sessions. Their participation and prior orientation to ROPE enhanced the students' experience and provided opportunities for carryover learning in the classroom. Most important, teachers gave up, and shared with an outside agency, coveted classroom teaching time. Their recognition of the importance of primary prevention allowed them to make way through the growing demands of "back to basics" and allow for a successful implementation of the project. Again, this is no minor point. One teacher's unwillingness to collaborate with and make a commitment to primary prevention can undermine and even extinguish this variety of primary prevention.

3. From the outset, there had to be an educational leader (in most cases, the school principal) who understood the importance of primary prevention and embraced it in the context of the Rite of Passage Experience. Again, in the absence of this administrative and conceptual support, the project never would have been initiated or sustained. Keep in mind that principals have a lot to say about how teachers use their time.

4. The professional resources required to facilitate a group place significant demands on a system for staff time. Each group of eleven to thirteen students requires at least two professionally trained staff members, or at least one highly skilled and specially trained volunteer and one professional staff member. Before the implementation of the Rite of Passage Experience, a group of twelve to fifteen guides, teachers, school administrative personnel, parents, special services staff, community agencies (such as police and Youth Service staff), and other significant persons participate in a five-day training. This training, for representatives of the schools, the community, and families, provides a critical foundation, with their support and understanding of the requirements and complexity of the primary prevention intervention. This core group is then able to become committed to and take responsibility for the

implementation of this primary prevention strategy. The core group is able to work in the community to build understanding of and recruit participation in the Rite of Passage Experience.

5. Parental involvement is critical to all phases of the Rite of Passage Experience. Parents' participation in the orientation and in several sessions supports, encourages, and is rewarding for students during the various challenges. Parental involvement not only is useful, it functionally and symbolically links parents and students during this important transitional period.

6. The school and the community have to make a financial commitment, not only for professional staff but also for the materials and equipment required for the Rite of Passage Experience. Although the actual cost for materials is minimal (somewhere in the neighborhood of ten to twelve dollars per student), limited financial resources may be a "good reason" why primary prevention strategies are not employed. Good reasons, like straw dogs, come in many varieties.

7. In this day and age of increased concern (more likely, dread) over liability, the insurance factor may provide another "good reason" for not employing the Rite of Passage Experience or similar endeavors. Even though implementation does not require all communities to provide rock climbing, rappelling, or similar challenges (alternative challenges may be successfully incorporated into the project), insurance questions offer a compelling argument against this strategy. A community's unwillingness to accept the importance of primary prevention precludes any commitment to procuring insurance or other necessary resources. But, even though there is a growing trend in the insurance industry to exclude coverage for such activities as rock climbing and rappelling, such coverage does remain available through some specialty markets and well-informed major insurance companies.

A fact to keep in mind is that according to national statistics produced from a review of millions of program days, activities such as rock climbing and rappelling are safer than downhill skiing, canoeing, and even camping in cabins at summer camp, not to mention scholastic football, soccer, and so on (Hale, 1988).

The size of ROPE groups requires that a typical class of twenty to thirty students be divided in half, and this means finding additional space. Many schools are now bursting at the seams, and it is interesting to note how poor planning contributed to the critical issue of space shortage. When the school population began to dip during the late 1970s and throughout the 1980s, school buildings were sold or converted (often to housing) in response to immediate conditions and the prospect of financial gain. But with the recent increase in the school-age population, the requirement for additional classrooms and special space for ROPE sessions places demands on school systems already struggling under the weight of tremendous expectations.

8. Successful implementation of a comprehensive primary prevention strategy, such as the Rite of Passage Experience, usually must receive a policy endorsement from the local board of education and local governmental body. A critical point here, and one not to be taken for granted, is that these two policymaking bodies must collaborate—again, no small task. Also important is the ability of each body to understand and appreciate the theoretical underpinnings of primary prevention and its economic and practical value to a community, especially when the need for primary prevention services is overshadowed by other essential demands. The only thing that happens when government or boards of education do not consider primary prevention strategies is that things gradually get worse or stay the same. The conflict between reacting to crisis or planning for the future and utilizing primary prevention strategies arises.

9. Endurance, patience, and time are essential to the successful implementation of a community intervention.

10. Acceptance of and participation in a process for program development and implementation is the last critical element. Viable prevention strategies are born and sustained from an ongoing process of collaboration. This occurs when communities reject simplistic quick fix measures that have proven to be inadequate. This important element also recognizes the dynamic nature of human interaction and the need to establish a structure for ongoing evaluation and modification of the intervention in order to meet the changing needs of a community.

One of the greatest challenges in the human services is harnessing and sustaining the creative spirit that gives rise to an idea for a new program. The energy and excitement that accompany creative new ideas carry one through in implementing new solutions to critical problems.

Moving beyond traditional, well-worn, and sometimes ineffectual service delivery methods necessitates thoughtful insights, which can lead to new and creative responses. The human services administrator or planner becomes a kind of artist, a creator stimulated by the constellation of dynamic relationships between theory and practice and between science and art. New ideas, whether translated through canvas, film, theater, and music or through human service delivery, go through a similar process. The outcome of a particular idea is shaped by intrapsychic and environmental forces. The musician hears the notes and the rhythm of a new song. This experience is exciting, energizing, and it fuels the production of a new artistic piece. The painter works feverishly, captured by a new thought. Artists are powerful receptors of new ways of hearing, seeing, and thinking. They work at their own pace.

But the spark of a new idea may be quickly extinguished in the social-political medium of human service delivery. Unlike other creative artists, the human service artist must contend with environmental forces unparalleled in any other creative field. Each new program idea undergoes a high degree of scrutiny and review by committee, which has extinguished many new ideas. Ideas for new programs may receive critical acclaim (administrative and policy endorsements) solely for their ability to fit into an existing administrative or financial structure.

Ten Minimum Conditions

Restated, the elements that can be considered the minimum conditions necessary for a comprehensive primary prevention strategy are the following:

1. Collaboration among the major environments that affect youth (school, community, and family), reflected in the formation and maintenance of a functional core group
2. Commitment to accepting that problems of living exist and to taking primary prevention seriously

3. Community and educational leaders with vision and a com-
    mitment to primary prevention
4. Personnel resources committed to primary prevention
5. Parental involvement in program development and imple-
    mentation
6. School and community financial commitment
7. Administrative support to secure insurance, equipment, space,
    and other program requirements
8. The school board's and local government's policy to support
    primary prevention
9. A keen understanding of the need for time, endurance, and
    patience
10. Acceptance of and participation in a process for program de-
    velopment and implementation

Note that these ten elements are very similar to those essential to the
success of a Youth Service Bureau (see Chapter Two).

Is It Worth Doing Anything if the
Minimum Conditions Do Not Exist?

The willingness and ability of a community to identify and evaluate
problems openly and honestly and then to collaborate in developing strategies to ameliorate them is the essential building block of
a comprehensive human service delivery mechanism. A *mechanism*,
in this instance, means the structure (Youth Service Bureau) or strategy (ROPE) established and created to provide services, especially
primary prevention services.

The Youth Service Bureau was established as a mechanism
for fostering collaboration in solving human problems. More often
than not, the absence of open, honest dialogue in a spirit of collaboration has maintained only mediocre human services, at best. It is
difficult to bring a new strategy or program into a community. It
cannot be overstated: implementing comprehensive primary prevention strategies is extremely complicated. Consider the energy,
time, and coordination of community resources necessary to link
every young person with a positive leisure-time activity (phase 2 of
ROPE) and engage youth in community service activities (phase 3

of ROPE). If the minimum conditions do not exist, does it pay to do anything?

What follows is a glimpse of what may confront a new idea— or, more accurately, an old idea in a new place. The case history is in no way intended to denigrate the process or the people involved. It is used here to illustrate the need for endurance, patience, and time and the need for collaboration. Here, of course, we must recognize that many new ideas are worth extinguishing, and there is merit in intensive review. The process of review and judgment of new human service ideas may be critical to ensuring that each new "wave" or "fad" does not become another community experiment.

The Wall

On June 3, 1987, Capel McCutcheon,* a handsome twenty-two-year-old man, was killed in a helicopter crash while training as a pilot. In his memory, and as the highest compliment that can be paid to any human service agency, his family established a memorial fund in his name in a community-based Youth Service Bureau.

Capel was spirited and adventurous. He had a lifelong battle with learning disabilities. His family remembered the joys and successes Capel had had in the Youth Service Bureau's camping and adventure programs. They wanted to support something that would allow other young people in the community to learn and experience the importance of the outdoors and adventure, as Capel had. Thus was born the idea of "Capel's Challenge," or "The Wall."

The wall should be made of wood and range from ten to fourteen feet high and ten to fourteen feet wide. It serves as a vehicle for a group challenge and for subsequent dialogue. A group is challenged to help all its members climb from one side of the wall to the other, with only the aid of the group. The wall is used as a strategy for helping participants develop trust, group problem-solving skills, cooperative behavior, and self-esteem while presenting a fun and exciting way to learn and gain a sense of accomplishment.

*In further remembrance and with permission of the family, I have used Capel's name.

In June 1987, the family submitted a proposal to the town's Recreation and Parks Department. The director of Recreation and Parks seemed to favor the proposal for placement of the wall in a public park, but such a proposal had to be reviewed by the Recreation and Parks advisory board. From June until the end of October, the Recreation and Parks advisory board had the proposal on its agenda. Board members discussed the proposal, questioning specific aspects (such as the appropriateness of the wall's placement in a public park, safety considerations, and insurance availability) and raising general concerns about use of the wall for young people in the community.

All issues, including the insurance issue, were successfully resolved, or so it was said. At the board's November meeting, the family gave a wonderful presentation about Capel and the wall. Nevertheless, the Recreation and Parks advisory board suggested to the family that the wall be constructed at a school, since it really served an educational purpose. The board then voted against the construction of the wall in a public park.

In November, the family submitted a proposal to the superintendent of schools, for the wall's placement at an elementary school. A particular school site was selected because of its central location in the town, its proximity to a park used in a youth program, and its fit with the existing playscape (an expansive wooden structure, like a jungle gym, used for climbing).

The proposed design was also modified to accommodate concerns about insurance and safety. The initial design included two ten-foot-wide walls, to be constructed in a V shape. One wall would be ten feet high, and the other would be fourteen feet high. This would provide a significant degree of flexibility in the use of the wall by different age groups. It was also as high as the existing playscape structure. The modified design was for one ten foot high by ten foot wide wall, with a safety platform on the back.

The insurance committee, the insurance agent, and other people in the insurance and safety field recommended that an eight-foot-high chain-link fence be constructed around the wall, to prevent anyone's unauthorized use. It became apparent that the community suspected that the wall would attract all kinds of unsafe activities, from which residents needed to be protected.

In early December, the superintendent of schools responded to the family's request. He said that a more appropriate place would be a park and refused permission to proceed.

Six months after the initial idea for construction of the wall, the proposal was at a standstill. The only wall being constructed was the one against the proposal. The family, concerned about and sensitive to the community's response, began to wonder whether there was some negative connotation of the wall as a memorial. More important, the family's "unfinished business" surrounding Capel's death remained unresolved.

In my capacity as Youth Service Bureau director, I continued to pursue an appropriate placement of the wall, now being referred to as the *McCutcheon Memorial* or *Capel's Challenge*. Meetings were conducted with officials from the town manager's office, the Building Department, the Community Development Department, the Engineering Department, and the Recreation and Parks Department. Members of the town council began asking questions, after months of reports documenting obstacles to the proposed structure. Finally, in the spring, a fifteen-acre parcel of town-owned open space was identified as available and appropriate for use. The land abutted an interstate highway and had been purchased by the town after completion of a federal and state highway.

There was elation. There were deed restrictions. There was deflation. After investigation by the Youth Service Bureau, the community development director, the chief engineering and building officials, and the town manager, it was determined that use of the land for "passive recreational purposes" was within acceptable deed restrictions. To be on the safe side, however, the State Department of Transportation, Office of Rights of Way, was approached for final approval.

In the beginning, there had been optimistic enthusiasm for the McCutcheon family's proposal. As each potential site became known, the family was quickly advised. With each elimination of a potential site, and with the subsequent letdowns, more caution was exercised in telling the family about available sites. The family was wonderful—patient and reserved in the obvious desire to see this project through.

In record time, the State Department of Transportation responded to this most recent request. Within two weeks, verbal notification was received from the director of the Office of Rights of Way. He approved the proposal for the use of the land. Family members were notified. There was elation. They were overjoyed and demonstrably appreciative of the efforts undertaken by the town on behalf of the memorial. Several weeks passed. Caution prevailed in the wait for written approval.

Finally, the letter arrived, and permission was granted. As I read the words granting permission, I felt great. Finally, we could move forward. I approached the last line of the letter, already thinking ahead to the next phase of construction. I read the last line again, bewildered.

Wide-eyed and panicked, I ran up three flights of stairs to the Engineering Department, clutching the letter. We spread out the land survey map. The building officials, community development director, and chief and deputy chief of engineering pored over the survey. We looked at the letter. We looked at the map. Eyes moved back and forth—letter, map, letter, map—as if we were watching a Ping-Pong match. No one spoke. My heart sank.

The letter's last sentence seemed to get larger and larger, almost jumping off the page: "It has been noted that there is no access to the property; therefore, please advise how the town would propose to enter for the intended use."

"Do you mean to tell me that the town bought fifteen acres of land from the state that we can't get to?" I asked, angry and confused.

Everyone shrugged simultaneously and said, "I guess so."

"There is one way you can access the land," the town engineer said, pointing to the map. "Over here, we can access through this resident's land."

The other members of the group nodded in endorsement of the engineer's observation. In disbelief, I left, clutching our last hope: the name and address of the property owner.

Telephone calls were made. Letters were written. Several conversations were held with the resident's son, in the attempt to help his father understand the nature of our problem. The resident, cordially but with sincere concern and fear, denied our request. We observed the one-year anniversary of Capel's death with this news, and there was no solution in sight.

By now, almost three dozen people had become involved, in one way or another, but the idea for this project had progressed only this far. With all objectivity, it should also be noted that many of those involved were helpful and sincerely interested in completing Capel's Challenge.

The State Department of Transportation was also helpful and suggested that we petition the federal government, which, with state support, would waive federal interstate highway access restrictions. The department was confident that permission would be granted, but it would take six months to a year. The wall against The Wall was getting higher and more difficult to vault.

I was tired and frustrated. I was resigned to entering our request to the Federal Department of Transportation and waiting it out. On behalf of the town, the town manager did not want to pursue this avenue. With a great deal of subjectivity, I will add that this attitude defied logic and seemed to indicate that the town would not pursue obtaining access to the land that it owned, even if the land was not exclusively for the construction of a wall. Embarrassed and dejected, we told the family of our predicament.

We turned once again to the town map, to identify several other potential sites. My resolve was undaunted. I walked almost every piece of open land in town. I was on a hunt, stalking the elusive parcel of usable land. Our prey was before us. A six-acre wooded parcel of open space was tracked. We called in the allied troops—town manager, engineering, building, and community development officials—to review deeds, land surveys, and the political climate. We received approval to proceed.

The land was in a high-rent district in town, bordered by a parcel of state highway land. We sent out letters to all the homeowners, advising them of our plan. The letter began, "As good neighbors, the town would like to advise you . . . ," and explained our intended use of the land.

We waited for a month. Two people called to clarify how the wall would be used. They were comforted and satisfied. No one objected. I did not get excited. We submitted an informal application to the Planning and Zoning Committee. We proposed that the wall be perpendicular to the main road and to the dozen homes that abutted the open space. That meant the wall would be built twenty yards into the woods, behind two homes on a dead-end road—the least intrusive and least noticeable placement. That seemed reasonable—until, of course, we were told that one of the two homes was owned by a member of the Planning and Zoning Committee. Approval came from the committee, with a restriction that the wall be placed parallel to the main road and positioned so that it would be least noticeable and intrusive for the home owned by the member of the committee. The restrictive language was not that precise, but the result was the same. I was not surprised. I was not excited. I was not suspicious or doubtful. I was tired.

Approval for construction of Capel's Challenge was given in September 1988, fifteen months after Capel's death and the presentation of the initial idea and proposal. Several weeks later, I received a call in the morning from members of the work crew, who said they had the materials to begin construction of the wall. They were ready to go. I hurried out to the land and marked off the site for the project. The date was October 4, sixteen months and one day after Capel's death. That afternoon, I returned to the site to see how work was progressing. To my surprise, no one was there. The woods were still. Before me stood the completed wall. It had taken less than a day to build.

On October 22, in the rain, family and friends held a dedication for Capel's Challenge. The mood was light and jovial. Everyone was noticeably pleased with the tribute to Capel. We all offered small remembrances of him. Then, almost spontaneously, friends and family worked together to help one another over the wall. A challenge was met. One wall was constructed, and many were torn down. We had learned many things—most notably, that it takes sixteen months and one day to build a ten-foot-by-ten-foot wall.

For the most part, nothing in our educational experience prepares us for understanding the time it takes for anything new to take hold and become embedded in a community. Whether it is a wall or any other community intervention or program, you cannot count on its being engineered according to a calendar.

This runs contrary to most early school or work experiences, which place heavy emphasis on accomplishing tasks within a certain period of time. Lessons are structured hour by hour and day by day, in an orderly progression; homework has to be done within twenty-four hours. Our early experiences teach us that completion of most tasks is inextricably linked to time. Our training is to work as quickly as possible to complete tasks.

Most social program funding sources (especially state and federal governments) set time boundaries without sufficient appreciation of the delicate balance between the birth of a new idea and the time it really takes to successfully embed it in a community. Funding criteria and availability generally overshadow and direct the development of new programs. (Consider what the outcome would have been if construction of the wall had depended on a grant with a one-year time constraint.) Forging collaborative relationships and identifying the critical elements of a new community intervention will take time and require significant patience and endurance on the part of those responsible for planning and implementing human service programs.

How is it that, in spite of all this, some communities are able to employ primary prevention strategies? Aside from the elements already discussed and described, what are the other critical elements to consider? How can a community request and successfully employ a primary prevention intervention?

10

§‧‧‧‧‧§

Primary Prevention:
Art or Science?

It must be said at the outset that we continue to know less than we could about how primary prevention interventions are successfully implemented and sustained in a community. This point may lead us to conclude that the act of constructing and delivering a primary prevention strategy has as much to do with art as with science, for if it were indeed a science, we could have a methodology or guidelines with which to replicate, over and over again, strategies that take hold and work well in some communities. If it were a science, we could, with relative certainty, predict every eventuality.

There are two things about which we can have some degree of certainty. First, there is a body of knowledge that can guide us in action. Second, everything in us prompts us to misevaluate what is going on in communities and in society. The confluence of these two ideas is evident in the art of constructing and delivering primary prevention community interventions.

For example, there is a body of knowledge that defines the production of paint colors. Mix blue and yellow, and you get green. This is predictable. But the application of the paint to produce a new work is art. The outcome of this application of color may not be so predictable.

Can we ever truly transfer a successful strategy from one community to another? The purpose of this book is to pursue answers to this and other questions, which I raise and believe to be critical in the attempt to plan and administer primary prevention community intervention strategies. The contents of this book are more a product of my own fumbling and relearning of the second point, about misevaluating what is going on in communities and in society (over and over again), than they are a recapitulation of any body of knowledge.

Can We Reproduce Primary Prevention?

A primary prevention community intervention is the systematic implementation of a comprehensive strategy that enhances environments and presents opportunities for young people to learn essential skills, attitudes, and beliefs. It also provides reasons for young people to believe that they can fit into society. It is delivered by many segments of a community to all youth at critical developmental stages. The strategy requires collaboration among four major constituencies—families, schools, the community, and youth. Effective comprehensive primary prevention strategies require a commitment from diverse representatives of a community. The community must also accept responsibility for implementing the strategy and share ownership and responsibility for helping all young people develop into healthy, happy, productive adults.

An example of a comprehensive primary prevention community intervention was provided in Part Two, to permit the reader to comprehend the complexity and difficulty of implementing this kind of strategy. We are not talking about a "quick fix" or a purely passive educational approach.

Uncovering the elements essential to constructing, delivering, and sustaining primary prevention community interventions requires careful attention. Questions like "How did this new idea get in here in the first place?" and "Who started this thing?" are important. How and by whom a primary prevention strategy is initiated in a community lays the foundation and is critical to the strategy's overall success and ability to be sustained over time.

As previously discussed, it is difficult to dictate any guiding set of principles or practices for successfully implementing and sustaining community interventions. Human interactions are complex, subtle, and subject to numerous elements that produce variations. In the previous chapter, we briefly examined ten minimum conditions essential to implementing and sustaining the primary prevention community intervention described in Part Two (see Chapter Nine). In this chapter, we shall examine how each of those ten critical elements shades and textures the planning, implementation, and maintenance of primary prevention community interventions.

Minimum Conditions, and a Little Luck

Initiating a community intervention is a lot like planning for conception (although the act itself is certainly not as pleasurable). Important relationships need to exist, from which the spark of an idea for a community intervention can grow into the plans for a successful program. Incubation of the idea for a new program must have certain life-sustaining nutrients available. Like conception, the start of a community intervention usually begins with two people who have an understanding of the community and are in a position to effect change.

An idea may exist somewhere outside the system (a school, a community, a residential facility) that ultimately provides the site (womb) for program planning and (prenatal) development. For example, someone in a community or a school system may have heard or read about a program in another locale. She gets excited about the possibility of replicating that idea within her own system. She shares the idea for the new program with other people in her system. In many cases, she never considers or asks what it took for that community or school to implement the new program and what minimum conditions had to exist before that program could begin. Even when she does pursue answers to these questions, her efforts may be lacking. She is usually pursuing answers to these difficult questions from a position of being constantly interrupted. Not only does everything in us prompt us to misevaluate what is going on in a community (and thus miss many predictable problems) but also there are a host of complex obstacles that converge on any new strategy implemented in a community.

Here we find magical thinking. Let us continue the metaphor of conception and birth. Failure to ask these important questions would be tantamount to having no understanding of how conception and birth occur. In the most extreme cases, it would mean assuming that there is divine intervention and virgin birth, and that programs can be magically transported from one location to another and implanted effortlessly in a community or school. Investigating and understanding how a system and an idea join for conception and birth is critical to the success and longevity of a community intervention.

Conception of an idea does not necessitate intimacy among and between consenting parties, but certain personal and environmental elements need to exist. The idea for a program is initially sustained by the enthusiasm, initiative, and strength of the principal participants in the program's conception. The moment when an idea for a new program is conceived is usually characterized by heightened enthusiasm and almost complete disregard for acknowledging, let alone discussing, predictable problems. It is almost like the heat of passion. If people sought to critically examine the complexities inherent in implementing the new program, the creative spark would soon be extinguished.

To avoid throwing the baby (new program idea) out with the bathwater, one must recognize that there is a trade-off. Utilizing the enthusiasm and energy created along with the birth of the new idea helps to sustain the effort through implementation. Yet, in the absence of thinking about and uncovering the problems likely to occur in a new program, there is a greater likelihood of stumbling during the subsequent stages of implementation. The long road to program birth is fraught with a veritable jungle of potential obstacles, which could serve to abort the idea or create a miscarriage in program implementation. In fact, it is almost certain that the implementation of the new program will not be exactly like the initial idea and will not correspond perfectly to the intent present on conception. Mutations during incubation do occur. In fact, some are beneficial to the overall implementation as the idea is refined to meet the unique needs of the community.

The Core Group

Unless they are well sown and cultivated, the seeds of a wonderful idea are doomed. During the development of a new idea for a program, one must consider who can play a principal or supporting role in its implementation. How can these people be identified and brought together in a process that nurtures the idea and gives it the best care, thus helping to bring it not only to birth but to a happy, long, productive life in the community?

Identifying and empowering a core group to manage the creation and implement the new idea is essential to building a solid foundation for the new creation to grow. The core group must have a diverse membership and be able to predict (as well as anyone can) and, even more important, accommodate emerging problems confronting the new intervention. A core group is committed to and takes responsibility for the implementation of the new initiative. Most of the ten crucial elements involve commitment from a wide variety of community representatives. Training for a primary prevention community intervention must recognize and be partly driven by the need to create a functioning "family" or core group.

Successful implementation of the Rite of Passage Experience, or of any other primary prevention community intervention, requires between twelve and fifteen persons from the community to be committed to participating in core-group training. In large cities, several interconnected core groups may represent distinct neighborhoods. Representatives from the schools, government, and community human service agencies (including policymakers, administrators, and direct service persons) are identified. They are all essential to the successful implementation of the strategy.

In the case of the Rite of Passage Experience, community representatives simulate the students' participation in this primary prevention strategy during a five-day training. The goal of this training is to ensure the successful transmission of important theoretical and practical aspects of the primary prevention intervention and to help promote stronger understanding, commitment, and appreciation. The training also creates a process in which participants engage in ongoing dialogue for the purpose of learning, refining, and sustaining the strategy while ensuring that responsibility for the success of the implementation clearly rests on the shoulders of the core group. The training moves participants toward interactions that produce increased ability for collaborative, problem-solving behavior. In almost all cases, the participants who complete the five-day training develop the fourteen important characteristics necessary in a functional core group.

Essential Ingredients of a Core Group

The essential ingredients that promote partnerships and facilitate core group functioning are the following:

1. *Trust*. There is an understanding that no one will try to hurt anyone else in the core group, especially in an attempt to accomplish the challenge of bringing the new idea to fruition. The group members have a commitment to ensuring one another's psychological and emotional safety. They have established an atmosphere conducive to working together and helping one another during the challenging task of program development and implementation. Experiential initiatives that contain elements of perceived risk for participants have been used extensively in promoting trust among group members. Trust, like all the other elements, should not be taken for granted. Although the need for it in creating and sustaining a core group is obvious, the harsh reality is that this is a most elusive element to create and maintain.

2. *Cooperation/Collaboration*. It should not be taken for granted that people have an innate ability or desire to work together for the successful outcome of a project, even when the project is critical to the mission of the organization or system. A fair number of wonderful ideas, as well as the daily operations of agencies, schools, governments, and all other systems and institutions, limp along in a competitive, antagonistic spirit. This is an important point, which business and industry are focusing on by building work teams and quality circles. It is erroneous to assume that because people work in the same institution or agency they will collaborate for the greater good of the organization. If people were inclined to collaborate, would we need a United Nations?

3. *Problem-Solving Skills*. Again, it would be a great mistake to assume that adults have adequate problem-solving skills. It would be even more erroneous to assume that they can employ adequate problem-solving skills in stressful situations. If all this were not enough, they also need to be able to utilize adequate problem-solving skills collectively. The first two elements, espe-

cially trust, are obviously critical to individual and group problem solving.

4. *Acceptance/Appreciation of Core Group Members' Uniqueness.* A core group brings together people from the community who have a wide variety of professional and personal skills, beliefs, attitudes, and abilities. Maximum utilization of this diverse group requires each member to recognize each individual's essential skills and abilities, which are important to the group's success. A functional core group must ensure or create an atmosphere in which each member is accepted as equally important and powerful. In a school or a community, group members may have different roles, which entitle them to different status and authority (a principal has more authority and higher status in a school than a teacher does). In the core group, a process must occur for all group members to be equally empowered, so as to foster greater opportunities for mutual appreciation and acceptance.

5. *Self-Esteem.* It is not uncommon for persons in the helping profession to overlook one another's basic needs. More common is their drive to create opportunities for helping young people or other identified populations develop healthy attitudes and beliefs about themselves and the world. Many times, however, this drive and subsequent behavior in performing a job may infringe on the basic needs of others. Feeling capable and good about oneself is crucial in a fully functioning person, who is essential to a fully functioning core group. Participation in the core group must offer an opportunity for all members to feel capable and good about themselves and thus enhance their self-esteem. When a system provides opportunities and rewards that enable fully functioning, capable individuals to perform their jobs, the mission of the organization is accomplished with greater success.

6. *Common Acceptance and Mutual Understanding.* With differing entry levels of acceptance and understanding (or comfortable confusion), the core group must build a uniform appreciation for the importance of primary prevention and its delivery through the context of a community intervention. Members must possess a working knowledge of and belief in the guiding principles of a given community intervention (for example, the Rite of Passage Experience). They must also understand and accept that an ongo-

ing, dynamic process is required for refining and revising a success-ful community intervention over time, to meet the changing de-mands of a particular community.

7. *Importance of All Members.* In keeping with the element of mutual acceptance and appreciation, all group members are es-sential to the overall success of the project implementation. Their implementation functions—whether as project staff (in the case of the Rite of Passage Experience, group facilitators or guides), admin-istrators, community liaisons, or representatives of other systems—must be accepted and seen as critical to the success of the project. When there is esprit de corps and acknowledgment that the core group is attempting something more important than the individ-uals in it, that members' efforts can make a significant difference in the future of many young people, and that each group member depends on each of the others for the successful implementation of the project, then each member can participate with a sense of im-portance and value.

8. *Desire of All Members to Be There.* Membership in any group carries with it rights and responsibilities, yet membership does not guarantee that the members want to be there. One has only to think about military conscription to understand this concept. On many occasions, and in critical situations, the members of a partic-ular group may have been "drafted." They may not fully accept and understand the purpose of the group and its mission or subscribe to the guiding principles of the group's task. Their physical pres-ence does not necessarily imply their full mental participation. Re-luctance in and resistance to participating will handicap the development of a functional core group and its overall ability to implement the project successfully.

9. *Maintenance of Enthusiasm.* The new idea is accompa-nied by energy and enthusiasm, which help bring the idea to devel-opment and implementation. Spreading, increasing, and sustaining the enthusiasm for the project is critical to its implementation. The new idea's spark ignites the core group, and members help carry the torch for the new project. Attention to the other essential elements of a core group, especially common understanding and mutual ac-ceptance of the project, helps motivation. Again, esprit de corps emerges and promotes an attitude that the project will be good for

students and fun to conduct. Fun, especially during the core group's training, is valuable in sustaining enthusiasm for the project. If we are to promote services that meet providers' basic needs, attention to fun is no small point. Children and youth are not the only people entitled to fun.

10. *Increased Ability for Intragroup Communication.* Enhanced group communication solidifies the foundation for several other important elements, including group problem solving and collaboration. Productive patterns of communication among group members have a better chance of emerging when opportunities for this outcome are created specifically. The initial focus of the core group is on engaging members in a process that promotes more effective communication. Generally, patterns of communication established outside familiar circumstances and typical situations may provide the best opportunities. For example, at the outset, the core group's training could engage members in some group problem-solving task, a simulation game, a group initiative, or some other interaction as a vehicle for dialogue. (The core group may participate in the "name game," as described elsewhere.) These activities are fun and promote useful patterns of communication in an effectively functioning group. More often than not, however, the initial phase of group work is leader-directed and not focused on promoting productive patterns of communiction.

11. *Personal and Professional Growth.* Group members must perceive their participation as contributing to their personal and professional growth. As with the element of self-esteem, participants must believe that their participation in the training and subsequent delivery of the community intervention is growth-enhancing. The training must provide all members with something that is personally and professionally rewarding. A dramatic example is Outward Bound's corporate and leadership training, whose participants report both personal growth and professional enhancement (Willis, 1985; Executives, 1970). Participants in the training for the Rite of Passage Experience report having learned skills that are transferable to the classroom (teachers) and home (teachers and parents). Motivation originates in and is directed by satisfaction of personal needs first, not professional responsibilities.

12. *Empowerment.* Collectively, the core group's members

are clearly placed in a leadership role for planning and developing the implementation of the community intervention. The core group is empowered to determine the key components of project implementation (policy, design, setting, and so on). Members also become experts in the theory and application of the primary prevention community intervention. This element relies heavily on the make-up of the core group and the segment of the community represented. Without school administrative personnel, community leaders, parents, teachers, and other significant supportive and influential participants, the element of empowerment becomes more difficult to actualize and utilize.

13. *Awareness of Members' Historical Contexts.* Each member of the core group comes from a place in the community where his or her status, authority, reputation, and role are established. A dialogue must be opened to acknowledge each member's place in the community and the impact of these historical contexts on individual participation, as well as on the overall ability of the core group. For example, how will group members who are police officers, principals, and teachers accommodate students' perceptions of them in a seemingly inconsistent role, that of Rite of Passage Experience group facilitator or guide? How will a group member who is a parent be considered an expert by the community in the particular community intervention strategy in which he or she has received training? How will principals relate to "their" teachers in the different way prescribed by the egalitarian esprit de corps established during the group process? Illustrations could go on. Failure to consider this element leaves the successful outcome of the community intervention to chance.

14. *A Mechanism to Sustain Growth and Preserve Continuity.* Once the other elements have been created and cultivated in the core group, a mechanism must be established to sustain and reinforce them. Initial training that uses a core group provides a context for the new strategy to grow, develop, and become embedded in the community. Often, initial efforts spent in training are not sustained. Failure to recognize the importance of continued meetings by the core group after implementation begins frequently undermines all the initial training efforts. Continued meetings are essential in assessing and revising the intervention and providing

for midcourse corrections. Most important, continued meetings provide a vehicle for building and strengthening the core group's functioning. It is a fact of life that people come and go in jobs. Community leaders sometimes move, principals get transferred, and parents no longer have children in a particular school. This contributes to discontinuity in the core group. How does one perpetuate the esprit de corps of an ever-changing core group? Continual expansion of group membership and retraining of participants will be useful in preserving continuity. Sensitivity to this critical issue is important.

Primary Prevention: A Process, Not a Program

Developing and sustaining a functioning core group by attending to the fourteen elements just described contributes to the potential for the new strategy to become successfully embedded in the community. Consideration of these elements may originate in the mind of the trainer or consultant or community leader, but, during training, the importance of understanding and paying attention to these elements should be clearly conveyed to all group members. Since changes in group composition are inevitable, it is essential that these fourteen elements be the cornerstone of group training.

The core group's structure provides the foundation and the mechanism for supporting the development and implementation of a primary prevention strategy. Furthermore, the core group is instrumental in ensuring that the strategy becomes institutionalized. Collectively, group members represent important constituencies: policymakers, "movers and shakers," administrators, parents, and program staff. They are empowered to control the destiny of the project while carrying the flame of enthusiasm. They are in a position to continually evaluate and revise the intervention to maintain its viability.

These fourteen elements should not be taken for granted and assumed to be present simply because people are working for the good of other people. In fact, these elements become much more important in schools, human service organizations, and other helping contexts because the task of delivering human services is so difficult. How can people help others unless the helpers themselves are happy and secure and believe that they are being supported and that their own needs are being met?

The importance of the fourteen elements may be obvious to some. More often than not, however, programs and helping strategies appear in communities after one or two people travel a hundred miles (experts and consultants always seem to be outside the community) for training, ride back to town on white horses, and try to "save the children" or other needy groups. This process is usually accompanied by great fanfare, which precedes the establishment of a task force, a select committee, or a blue-ribbon panel to study, investigate, or review something. This distinguished group, serving in the capacity of scout, sends the troops out to bring back the magic solution.

Far too often, a community designates persons or systems—youth workers, crisis counselors, teachers, schools—to take responsibility for helping to raise young people and for responding to the necessary crises of adolescence. But successful strategies for helping youth across the threshold of adolescence and into adulthood require the participation of the entire community, which must become active and responsible. We can no longer afford to pay others to raise our children. The cost, in terms of drug and alcohol abuse, delinquency, depression, and suicide alone, not to mention a whole host of other intensifying problems, is too high.

Developing and implementing strategies that help people is a complex thing, unlike manufacturing widgets on an assembly line. Yet the assembly-line mentality places maximum importance on the packaged product or program, rather than on the process for promoting change and improving the human condition. This attitude is characterized by comments like "We've got to do something about this problem. Get a program in here, quick!"

Greater emphasis must be placed on an intervention as an ongoing process. An intervention cannot be effective if it consists of a stagnant program, forever unchanged. A "quick fix" may be politically expedient. It may fall within budget guidelines and ease the consciences of those who are responsible for helping people. But will it really help people? Will it remedy any of the problems that people face?

PART III

Primary Prevention Training in Communities

11

A Model Intervention

It is useful, at this point, to set out some points of reference, some markers to aid a community in its navigation through challenging waters to implement a primary prevention community intervention. I have characterized the case studies in the chapters that follow as a series of voyages. I have found that the use of this metaphor helps people see this enterprise in a new light.

The case studies illustrate the various ways in which communities have tried to implement the intervention strategy called the Rite of Passage Experience. The illustrations clearly reflect the importance of significant relationships—in a community, and as an essential minimum condition. Although the case studies report on replications of the Rite of Passage Experience, the considerations highlighted are essential to the implementation of any comprehensive primary prevention community intervention. When primary prevention is judged essential and is endorsed by a wide segment of the community, then and only then can prevention efforts become successfully institutionalized in a community. When a community utilizes a core group to nurture and implement a prevention strategy, the strategy continues to be dynamic and grows with the community's needs.

All the persons and communities used as examples had the best of intentions. The results were more a function of my misunderstanding, misevaluating, and failing to recognize important elements than of anything that anyone else did. In fact, only after repeated false starts, failures, and dramatic mishaps did I see a consistent theme emerging that could explain why things were not going as desired. Some community interventions were launched beautifully and remained gloriously afloat. Today they are helping thousands of people. Others sank or never even left the dock. I attempted to reconstruct the courses that led to these undesirable outcomes. What became quite apparent was that in implementation one or more essential elements had been ignored. To respect the desire for anonymity, I have changed names and altered events slightly, although essential characteristics remain unchanged. The descriptions are intended purely to enhance learning about training and implementation in primary prevention community interventions. Failure to bring community intervention strategy to fruition has had more to do with my inadequacies than anything else. Conversely, success had everything to do with the core group and its ability to help the new idea grow and become embedded in the community.

Only recently has it become clear to me that thinking about and planning for an intervention, as well as subsequent attempts to implement it in a community, is not like ordering textbooks or bringing in a new academic curriculum. You have to "case the joint" to ensure that the minimum conditions exist for a community intervention. This takes time. Unfortunately, human service delivery relies heavily on the availability of funding and on the fiscal year. Typically, funds have to be requested and spent very quickly, in contrast to the natural, desirable order of things when it comes to planning and implementing primary prevention community interventions. A critical question is how time becomes an important variable in an intervention's success or failure. Four guiding principles are important to keep in mind. First, someone looking for something wants to find it as soon as possible. Second, people who want to do something want to do it now. Third, when funding becomes available, grant applications must be submitted on time. Fourth, collaborative relationships may exist on paper but not in practice. Misunderstanding of these four points may undermine effective implementation.

A Pleasure Cruise

My phone rang. Dean Masters, director of Main Street Community Services, introduced himself and inquired about the Rite of Passage Experience.

"I've heard real good things about ROPE and would like to see if we can get it going here," he began.

"Fine. I'm glad that you've heard good things about the Rite of Passage Experience."

In the human services, a rose by any other name does *not* smell as sweet.

When initial discussions about the project use the name *ROPE*, people are misled into believing the project is like Outward Bound or other adventure-type programs. It is certainly anything but that. Right from the start, I must orient people to the nature of primary prevention strategies and the importance of thoughtful, deliberate intervention descriptions.

"The primary prevention community intervention is most effective," I continued, "when representatives from the community participate in a training. In this way, the people responsible for the delivery of the primary prevention strategy and those necessary to administer, support, and sustain the strategy all have a thorough understanding of the principles of primary prevention and the strategy of the Rite of Passage Experience. Most important, they take responsibility for its successful implementation."

"What kinds of representatives? Who?" Dean asked.

"Community-based youth service staff, school teachers, principals, special services staff, parents, police, government officials, town council members, and the board of education. People who directly serve youth and those who are in administrative and policymaking positions," I responded.

I went on to explain the three phases of training. First, a community presentation gives as many people as possible an overview of the problems, as well as an understanding of the concept of primary prevention and of rites of passage in ancient cultures. Second, a five-day training is conducted with ten to fifteen community representatives, who will become the core group. They will be directly involved in the delivery of the intervention. Third, follow-up consultation and training are provided to the core group and others. Here, people review the first phase of implementation. Additional consultation is available to assist with the development of the second and third phases.

"Well, where do we go from here?" Dean asked when I had finished.

"I can send you some information to help orient you. You can share it with people you feel would be interested and able to help."

"Okay. That would be really helpful. Do you think we could set up a community presentation?"

"Sure. But first, why don't we see what the response is to this information in your community?"

I was somewhat hopeful, but I wondered if Dean really got it. Did he really understand how complex this whole thing is?

The Port of Entry

Main Street Community Services was a youth/family service agency in a medium-size, blue-collar city with a solid industrial base and an interracial population. "Clean Dean," as he came affectionately to be known, was a dynamo whose contacts in the community were wide. He was well respected, not only in the community where he worked and lived but also across the state. His strong political and professional contacts became keys to his ability to coordinate community involvement in training and implementation of ROPE. His membership in civic service organizations and community recreational athletic leagues, as well as his good nature, caring, and history of outstanding community service, contributed to his ability to move easily among different groups. Police, school, clergy, business, civic and community organizations all recognized and respected his position. More important, people liked him as a person. Suffice it to say that Dean understood how to access the keys to the city, which made this community a clear, friendly harbor.

The place of first contact in a community—the "port of entry"—is important. When a large ship approaches a harbor, a harbor pilot comes on board the vessel to navigate it into port and help it dock safely. The harbor pilot knows the harbor well and is skilled at navigating through its waters. In the same way, the success of a community intervention rests on the skills and knowledge of the community coordinating agent who serves in the role of harbor pilot. Dean was the consummate harbor pilot. His knowledge about the community kept the project off the rocks. He maintained a solid course, slowly and skillfully moving the project through the proper channels and safely into port.

Regardless of Dean's skill and knowledge of the community, he could not have been so successful with the implementation of ROPE had it not been for Dan Ross. Dan was the principal of an elementary school in the community. Dan and Dean had worked together on other projects and had a very good relationship. Dean brought the idea into the community, and Dan had the place for its trial run. Dan was as enthusiastic as Dean was about the idea of a modern-day rite of passage. In part, the minimum conditions existed in the working relationship between Dean and Dan. Their mutual understanding of the importance of ROPE, their enthusiasm for the intervention, and their desire to see it in their community were essential ingredients in its successful implementation. This is no minor point. In the absence of two or more persons' ability to collaborate and bring a program idea to port in a community, even the best ideas, the best community interventions, will sink.

Dean was not alone in piloting ROPE into the community. Almost from the beginning, Dan was there with him, serving as a key link to the educational community. Together, they were able to carefully evaluate the community's resources and the potential pitfalls in implementation. In a sense, they were able to "case the joint," to investigate the most effective and easiest port of entry for the project.

Dean's agency would be doing the yeoman's share of the implementation work. Along with Dean, two youth counselors, Mary and Richard, would be the core of the direct service implementation team. They were also enthusiastic about the intervention and had prior knowledge of and positive attitudes toward experiential techniques. The core group was beginning to form.

Let me make a distinction here about the core group. Diversified membership in the core group is essential to the success of a community intervention. A key ingredient for the success of this program, or almost any program that is effective, is the involvement of the widest possible representation of the community. This factor may be the single most important reason why we have not made significant strides in affecting our children's development through primary prevention efforts.

The first hazard loomed on the horizon: how to involve the teachers whose students would be participating in ROPE. Many teachers, for good reasons, are reluctant to participate in activities that fall outside the scope of the perceived responsibilities of traditional education. Teachers already see their responsibilities expanding, in response to the changes in society and the problems that children face. Involving teachers and other school personnel in primary prevention strategies is therefore a significant challenge, one that requires care and skillful navigation. It was both a quirk of fate and a large piece of luck that Dan was the principal of a new elementary school in the community—new in the sense that a reorganization of the school system had required the transfer of teachers from different schools to this one. A new constellation of characters—school personnel—set the context for a whole new set of opportunities. Dan thought that he could seize this opportunity to try something new and different, and he was right. Three teachers agreed to participate in the five-day training and pilot ROPE in their sixth-grade classes.

The three teachers were seasoned veterans, each with fifteen to twenty-five years' experience. It was quite apparent from the very first day of training that each was a dedicated, caring, competent, and fun-loving person. They had all been given limited information about ROPE and knew only that it was good and fun for students. They accepted the idea of rituals of initiation. Even more important, they were willing to take a risk and try something new.

When I think of this core group and how to characterize its members' enthusiasm and desire to bring something new and exciting to students, I remember the second day of training. It was a winter day. The morning session would be outdoors and present a challenge of orienteering—how to use a compass in the woods.

Coffee and doughnuts in hand, the group stood in the parking lot of a park at eight in the morning. Laughter and attempts to keep warm occupied attention as we began the training for orienteering. The weather forecast called for light snow. The sky darkened as we finished instruction and practice. By nine, the group was ready to break up into small triads and attempt an orienteering course set up in the woods.

The snow arrived shortly after the small groups set off. Half an hour later, it had turned into a blizzard. For almost an hour, in blinding snow, the teachers, the principal, and the agency staff trudged through the course. They returned to the parking lot with their entire bodies caked in snow. At this point, the training—in fact, the entire project—could have been lost.

"Let's get out of here and head back to the school!" Barbara, one of the teachers, called.

"I'm with you," Dan said.

The group members furiously cleared snow from their cars and drove off. When the parade of cars containing the snow-caked ROPE trainees pulled into the school parking lot, they were greeted by a line of school buses. Students were pouring out of the school, escorted by teachers. School had been cancelled because of the snow. The students and the teachers stood with their mouths open as the ROPE trainees filed past.

"Hey, Mrs. Jones! What were you doing?" one of the students yelled.

Mrs. Jones called back, "We were learning something real special, to do with our school."

"Oh, neat!" the student said.

Other school staff looked on, shaking their heads and grinning as the buses continued to load the departing students. The training group reassembled in one of the classrooms.

"We've got a problem here," Dan said. "I can't ask these teachers to stay when the schools have been closed."

The group was quiet for about five seconds. The members looked at one another.

"Well, let's stay. We can stay, right?" Mrs. Jones said. She was a twenty-five-year teaching veteran and a feisty mother of nine.

"If we just found our way through that orienteering course in this snow, we can do anything!" Mr. Jefferson, another teacher, exclaimed, to the laughter of the group.

Unanimously, the group nodded, and the trainees erupted in boisterous laughter, recalling their exploits in the woods.

At the end of the day, Dan called me aside and said, "I don't know if you are aware of how significant today was."

I shrugged, not sure what he meant.

"It was really rather incredible that the teachers decided to stay for the entire day," he said. "We have a unique group here."

Indeed, this was a unique group of caring, dedicated professionals committed to helping their students as much as they could. The training had helped promote commitment, collaboration among participants, and an understanding of primary prevention and the purpose of initiation rituals while fostering the development of ingredients essential to the formation of a core group. As luck would have it, the teachers returned to school during the snowstorm, in full view of the rest of the school, and this created a tremendous interest in ROPE throughout the school. A positive context and a nurturing environment were beginning to emerge in support of the new project.

After the five-day training, the teachers, the principal, the agency staff, and the administrator formed the majority of the core group. The pilot implementation of ROPE, several weeks later, was a resounding success. Students were given pre- and posttests to assess behavior, attitude changes, and other project goals. Teachers, agency staff, and parents answered a series of questionnaires to assess their perceptions of ROPE's impact on the students.

The first implementation of ROPE provided opportunities for parental participation, both before and after delivery of the program. The majority of the parents attended the orientation and follow-up sessions. The follow-up sessions gave the students an opportunity to share their experiences with their parents by showing them a slide presentation of their ROPE groups' activities while describing how they had felt and what they had learned during each session of ROPE.

When it came time to decide whether to adopt the project systemwide, several parents participated with the core group to promote ROPE in the community. Although the parents had not participated in the formation of the core group, their advocacy of the project was essential during the difficult task of selling the project to the policymakers—the board of education and the town council.

It is very difficult to convey, through the written or spoken word, what experiential learning entails. Even more difficult is conveying how the context and the process of a strategy are critical to its success. A typical policy-level question was Why can't you have one teacher do ROPE with an entire class? This would have been patently impossible, not to mention unsafe. Concern at the policy level was for budgetary considerations and, in general, programs' fit with policy and educational requirements; rituals of initiation probably sounded more like voodoo than like anything remotely connected with education.

Nevertheless, as luck would have it, an influential member of the town council understood something about experiential techniques. Dean Masters saw an opportunity in this fact, and he recommended that the entire town council go on a rock-climbing and rappelling outing to get a clearer understanding of what students would experience in ROPE. With a full media entourage, the majority of the council went climbing and rappelling for a full day with the agency staff. The next day's front page, with large photographs of council members at various stages of going up and coming down the cliffs, secured support for ROPE. The council's support was instrumental in obtaining the board of education's support for a gradual systemwide implementation of ROPE. More than six years later, almost five hundred sixth graders in ten elementary schools participate in the Rite of Passage Experience, which enjoys full community support.

What Have We Learned?

In no way was it apparent to me, years ago, that certain conditions had to exist before a community intervention could become successful and positively embedded in a community. Only when we experienced several project disasters and "sinkings" in certain communities did we realize that some important factors required our attention. In the absence of these minimum conditions, serious consideration should be given to not doing anything. Too often, we believe that the merits of an idea should carry it to successful implementation in a community. Idea after idea, generating program after program, invades a community with no relevant context and no real support.

In the example just discussed, the idea for the intervention was proposed by a well-respected, skilled professional, who had a long, successful history and many important links in the community. Second, an elementary school principal was enlisted and enthusiastically embraced the project. The two worked side by side to develop a core group. Third, agency staff, teachers, and administrators from both groups were included in a training, which ensured their understanding of the strategy and solidified their commitment to its implementation. The training created a bond among the group members, built on trust, mutual acceptance, and mutual respect. The importance of the relationship among the core group members cannot be understated. Their willingness to be involved in the project, as shown by their remaining at school during the snowstorm, and their continued involvement with one another was essential.

The training moved the group toward interactions that increased the ability for collaborative, problem-solving behavior. The fourteen elements necessary to a functional core group (see Chapter Ten) were clearly present here.

Once the core group had coalesced, its members were able to move the intervention toward successful implementation in the community. They were able to attend to, handle, and, in many cases, secure the ten elements describe in Chapter Nine.

In many ways, training focused as much on the process necessary for implementing and sustaining the project as it did on delivering ROPE to students. Again, this is no small point. It is a waste of time to prepare people to deliver a strategy if there is no process for evaluating, revising, and sustaining it. A strategy's capacity for significant positive impact on a community over time is limited if such a process is lacking.

It took this community over six years to implement the project systemwide. Over the years, it became clear that the creation of the core group had been critical to the success and survival of the intervention. The diverse core group also empowered people to modify and refine the strategy, tailor it to the changing needs of the community, share responsibility for its implementation, and coordinate the implementation of the second and third phases of the Rite of Passage Experience. Again, the key point is that the community took responsibility for planning, implementing, and sustaining this primary prevention strategy.

A program does not just land in a community and survive. To stay vibrant and alive, it must be cared for continually and modified as necessary. Given the minimum conditions and a little luck, the core group can ensure the project's success. A dedicated and diverse team of community representatives, committed to learning a strategy and the skills to create something positive, really can move mountains.

12

The Misevaluation of Communities

Only after we had run aground or sunk several times did it become painfully obvious when the minimum conditions did not exist. On several occasions, there had been inadequate attention to the development of a core group, and other essential ingredients were also missing. In a few cases, it would have wasted a lot less time and money to have done nothing at all.

It is from those failed attempts, scattered across the country, that we learned the most. I humbly include a discussion of my worst shipwrecks: interventions that wound up on the rocks while entering communities' ports; implementations that were torpedoed and sank; implementations that sailed off into the sunset in a completely different form from what had been intended (in those cases, what had begun as a primary prevention community intervention ended up as an after-school program loosely based on the original Rite of Passage Experience model).

Again, the failures resulted more from my inability to note the obvious than from anything done (or not done) by others. I can legitimately bask in the cool glow of failure, comforted by the knowledge gained from each of these mishaps.

A Shipwreck

I received a call one day from Don, the executive director of a large mental health center serving a medium-size Southwestern city. He discussed his agency's involvement with the city and its desire to replicate the Rite of Passage Experience. We had a lengthy exchange about the process of the project and the importance of training a diverse core group. The discussion kept returning to this question: "When can we get started? I have some grant money available right now."

Pleased by Don's obvious enthusiasm, I overlooked the significance of the money's immediate availability and simply established a training date.

As the time for the training approached, there were more conversations with Don and with Mark, a program coordinator. It became clear that we were not all on the same wavelength. Don stressed his agency's coordination and administrative role, while Mark kept describing his staff's program responsibilities. I continued to emphasize the core group's function and the importance of obtaining the widest community representation. I sent information about the total six-year, three-phase process of the Rite of Passage Experience. In retrospect, it is clear that none of us were talking about the same thing. Moreover, I completely missed their continued insistence on getting started because they had the money.

Several weeks before the training, I began to receive the pre-training information forms from the prospective participants. On one of the forms, there is a space to insert the name of the agency authorized to conduct the Rite of Passage Experience. It turned out that Don and Mark did not work at the same agency, although they did work in the same community. I noticed that six different agencies were listed on the forms. It soon became clear that six agencies in all, from four different communities, were participating in the training.

The agency where Don worked had had an opportunity to apply for funding. One stipulation of the funding was that several community agencies—suburban and, particularly, urban minority population–serving agencies—participate together. Mark's agency would be responsible for providing program coordination through funding of a staff position. Don's agency would receive funding only for administrative support (it was never clear what administrative support meant, except cashing the grant disbursement checks and keeping some money). Two other agencies, representing two smaller suburban communities, also participated, as did two urban minority population–serving agencies. This composition, I gathered, fulfilled the grant requirements.

No one but Don, Mark, and Bob, the program coordinator hired for the project, knew the particulars of the grant. Even worse, by the time I arrived for the training, it became evident that none of the participants knew anything about the Rite of Passage Experience, primary prevention, or why they were there in the first place. As we began to share our names and expectations of the training, one woman announced indignantly, "My supervisor told me to come here today."

It did not get any better as the participants introduced themselves and questioned, in many different ways, why they were all there. Here were the consequences of not adequately "casing the joint." I was not prepared to compensate for the fact that the participants were not from the same community, had no prior information about the goals and process of the Rite of Passage Experience, and had their own rather negative agenda and expectations.

Rather than ignore the fact that a storm was brewing, I prepared to batten down the hatches and sail right into the heart of the storm as best I could. I explained our precarious position and provided an overview of the Rite of Passage Experience, primary prevention, and the strategy of a community intervention. Although this did little initially to quell the gale-force storm of anger and hostility, it did offer a foundation for dialogue. After several hours, during which the participants vented their frustration and developed understanding about why we were there and what we could and could not do, the storm began to subside.

It was clear from the participants' contributions that a well-established historical context had shaped the early atmosphere of the training. The large, and generally white, mental health center had received many grants in the past. The smaller minority population–serving agency's perception was that the mental health center was not adequately serving the minority population but was getting all the money. The suburban communities, although aware of the issues presented by the smaller agencies, had their own issue surrounding alleged inequities and disbursement of grant funds.

The white, African American, Hispanic, Native American, male, and female participants in the training—eleven in all—were in no way on the verge of becoming a core group; quite the opposite. I was certain that there would be mutiny any second.

The port of entry was mined with deadly obstacles. There was no harbor pilot. Don and Mark were nowhere to be found. Poor Bob was looking for a life preserver. He had had no idea that there would be such strong negative sentiment toward his agency, the training, and the project.

A woman named Gloria spoke up in the midst of the griping. "Well, look, I for one don't want to sit around for the next five days and bitch and moan about this and that!"

"I'm sure there are some things we could get out of this training. We might as well make the most of it," Marie quickly added.

Several of the other participants agreed to move forward with the training. There was a growing consensus: the participants were resigned to being there, a huge first step. Over the next several days, the process of the training began to break through the participants' mistrust, anger, misunderstanding, and general feeling of disconnection and impotence.

The participants initially believed that they would not be able to implement the project without administrative participation and support. Once the group accepted (even if not enthusiastically, at first) that they would participate in the training, a host of opportunities emerged. When the participants had a better understanding of the community intervention strategy and had gained the skills necessary to implement ROPE, they began to develop the characteristics essential to a core group. By and large, the participants were dedicated, caring people struggling with the confusion and inadequacy of the system. As they coalesced into a core group, they began to characterize their challenge as "battling the system in order to implement the program." They became determined that they would prevail and that the project would be implemented successfully. At the end of the five-day training, they "demanded" to meet with the agency administrators and tell them what was needed to make the implementation a success.

The core group did not contain a single administrator, and

only one of the suburban communities had sent anyone from a school, but the group did manage to offer the first phase of ROPE in a variety of successful after-school projects. In fact, one of the suburban communities that had sent a school representative was able to conduct a very successful in-school program.

Several years later, we were called back to each of the suburban communities to provide training for administrators and parents. Several of the smaller agencies from the city had broken ties with the large mental health center and were able to secure more funding for further implementations of ROPE. There were no efforts in the city to coordinate a more strategic, systemwide application of the project. (Cities tend to present a more difficult port of entry in general.)

Without adequately "casing the joint"—assessing whether and how minimum conditions can enable this type of training process—one is liable to find a multitude of surprises. In fact, even when one thoroughly assesses the community and determines that the minimum conditions exist, one will undoubtedly encounter problems and obstacles that one never imagined. It is best to carefully find one's bearings and enlist a good harbor pilot.

In the case under discussion, the pilots abandoned ship at the mouth of the harbor. Don and Mark failed to participate in the training themselves and did not adequately prepare participants or participating agencies for anything that was to come. They cast the new idea into a sea of confusion, in a storm of controversy. It was only the caring and the sense of obligation of the core group that helped keep the project from sinking completely. But caring and obligation alone do not constitute minimum conditions.

In the absence of community support and administrative participation, even the best idea for a community intervention strategy cannot be implemented by a few trained, well-intentioned professionals. I am always fascinated by the wide array of permutations that occur during project implementations, after consultation and training. This particular consultation and training "event" made me painfully aware of the limitations and parameters of being a consultant.

No amount of information would have altered the agenda of Don and Mark: to bring the program in so that they could get the money. It did not matter how often I spoke about community coordination and participation. The grant required a certain type of agency and community participation, and that is just what Don and Mark were going to provide—no more, no less. There are no laws, regulations, or moral and ethical directives that say anyone has to do what consultants recommend or train people to do. We cannot expect people to collaborate just because we make it a stipulation for a grant. We cannot make people work together, no matter how much money we throw at them.

Human interactions are dynamic. In the context of a community, they are particularly volatile. Inter- and intracommunity systems' politics, peculiarities, policies, and practices contribute to the difficulty of assessing whether the minimum conditions exist in a community or ever could. Even when the minimum conditions do exist, there is no guarantee that an intervention will be a success and survive. There is nothing more predictable than a community's ability to be unpredictable. This idea and its cousin—the notion that if there is no logical reason why something should not happen, it won't—set the stage for the next illustration.

13

❧

Managing
the Unpredictable

After several years and hundreds of requests for information about
the Rite of Passage Experience, my responses became less enthusiastic and more skeptical. Time and again, similar comments followed our inquiries to communities that requested information.

"It sounds like a great program. We've heard really good
things about it, but it's too difficult to do."

"We couldn't possibly get all these people involved."

"Do you think a teacher could do it for a whole class?"

"Who builds the ropes course?"

It became extremely disheartening, in the face of many successful replications and extensive research that substantiated the
strategy's effectiveness, as well as hundreds of testimonials, to go on
explaining the intricacies of the Rite of Passage Experience. I was
confronted over and over with the "pill" or "slogan" mentality,
which tends to seek simplistic solutions to very complex human
problems.

The Officers' Mutiny

In this context, I was relieved to receive a call from Joan Glass, a
program coordinator from a well-established youth-serving agency.
Joan spoke with surprising understanding about the community intervention strategy and cited several sources on rituals of initiation.

"We have the principal of the elementary school, the head of the school's PTA and another parent, the school social worker, the director of my agency, and several other youth counselors, plus two other agencies, committed to participating in the community training," Joan said, very pleased and certain of her community's readiness.

"Are we talking about people who all live or work in the same community?" I asked, eager not to make the same mistake twice.

"Yes."

"Good," I said with relief. I still was not convinced that the minimum conditions existed, but at least we were talking about one community. "I wonder if it would be worthwhile to present an orientation about the concept of primary prevention and the Rite of Passage Experience for the teachers and others who would be involved in the training."

The orientation went well. The three sixth-grade teachers whose students would be in the first implementation were present. They seemed to be very familiar with and supportive of experiential techniques and the ROPE strategy. Although the teachers were not going to participate in the training, because of a conflict in their schedules, their understanding and verbal support eased my apprehension somewhat.

The training was scheduled for the summer, with fall implementation planned for the students. At the time, it appeared that the five-day training had gone well. Parents, the community agency staff and administrator, school social workers, and the principal were all enrolled. There were fourteen people in all, a perfect composition for the development of a core group. During the training, the group coalesced and worked extremely well. Members obviously enjoyed one anothers' company and clearly began to develop the characteristics essential to a functional core group.

Hindsight is always 20/20. What did not present obvious difficulty at the time should have been an indication of a predictable problem. Both the principal and the community agency administrator vanished periodically during the training, although this was not especially disruptive. "Called away to handle something" was the usual reason for these absences. But the training was going so well, and their verbal support and enthusiastic participation when they were present was so evident, that I overlooked the obvious.

Call it fate or bad luck, but several factors converged to undermine the implementation. Just as school was beginning, the principal had a heart attack. Critically ill, he was in the hospital and convalescing at home for several months. Needless to say, his return to school was very difficult, and implementation of ROPE was moved onto the back burner. During the summer, some mysterious personal problem removed one of the sixth-grade teachers from teaching, and another one retired.

The community-based agency serving as coordinator of the project patiently endured the turmoil and waited for the school to become ready for the implementation.

"Something is different about Pete," Joan said, trying to explain the marked change in the principal's attitude toward implementation of ROPE. "He is just not really back into school. His heart attack and the situation with the sixth-grade teachers is making him really anxious about the implementation. It's almost like he doesn't want to do it."

The agency administrator did not want to intervene and assist with moving the implementation forward. He was still functioning in the "called away to handle something" mode and believed that the school was the principal's territory: "He knows best." So much for empowerment of the core group to direct the implementation.

Joan and I agreed to suggest another orientation for the new sixth-grade teachers, which would also serve to reenergize the core group and sustain its growth. The principal did not want to do this. He instructed the teachers—who knew virtually nothing about ROPE except that it would be using "valuable class time," as they put it—to separate the classes into ROPE groups, with twelve students each.

Undaunted, the community-based agency rallied and, with a resurgence of enthusiasm, began the implementation. The principal even helped facilitate one of the groups. Throughout the implementation, teachers complained about the interruption of class time.

"I can't wait until this darn ROPE thing is over with," one

of the teachers announced in front of the entire class when one of the groups excitedly returned to class after a ROPE session.

"Why are they so excited when they return to class? I can't get anywhere with them after they come back. Can't you control these kids?" another teacher asked one of the ROPE facilitators from the community-based agency.

To make matters worse (if that was possible), one of these two teachers put twelve special-education students, diagnosed as emotionally disturbed, in one group and never told the group facilitators. This group lagged noticeably behind the other groups in level of participation. Both facilitators, looking for a reason, uncovered this fact.

The teachers' constant complaints to the principal wore him down. No longer willing to confront these two teachers, even in the face of students' and parents' positive evaluations of ROPE, the principal chose not to continue any more implementations. He did not want to discuss the matter and disallowed any effort to reassemble the core group so that it could examine what had happened— undermining the empowerment of the group, and denying its responsibility for the implementation. He also continued to thwart any efforts for the core group to meet, when meetings would have served as a mechanism to sustain growth.

———————————

What had happened?

After what seemed to be a flawless training, and with what seemed like the perfect core group, except for the absence of the teachers, the project sank miserably. As obvious as it appeared later, I completely failed to grasp that limited information and involvement on the part of the teachers would have that large an impact. Of course, there was no way to predict that two of the three teachers who had originally supported ROPE would no longer be teachers. (Again, the only thing predictable in a community may be that the unpredictable will probably happen.) This situation illustrates the critical issue of continuity. Given the tendency for people and systems to change, how does one maintain continuity?

The educational leaders once present and initially supportive, had receded in the wake of a complex series of personal and systemic problems. The community-based agency, and especially its administrator, did not want to tread on the turf of the elementary school and its principal. The context of the intervention ceased to be both the community and the school; it was transferred completely to the school, and authority for implementation, once residing with the core group, became the sole purview of the principal. There was limited commitment on the part of administrative staff, and there was no commitment from policymakers in the community, to employ a primary prevention strategy. Once again, grant funds were available to establish the project, and this fact limited the financial commitment of the community. It also limited the community's resolve and commitment to responsibility for sustaining a primary prevention strategy.

One way to view these events concerns the possibility that extenuating circumstances, extremely stressful not only for the principal but also for key members of the core group, precipitated a regression in the function of the core group. The recommendation for an orientation directed at the new teachers and for reenergizing the core group was rejected by the principal. This decision effectively neutralized the core group's ability to collaborate and take responsibility for the implementation.

Memories of the warm days of summer and of the participants' experiences during formation of the core group had waned by winter. As service and organizational demands from the school system and the community became overwhelming for key members of the core group, energy and efforts for implementation also waned. The Rite of Passage Experience lay at the bottom of the community's harbor. Eight of the ten minimum conditions for successful implementation were limited or completely absent:

1. Educational and community leadership
2. Administrative support
3. Local governmental and educational policy making bodies collaborate to endorse and support a primary prevention community intervention
4. Commitment and involvement of teachers
5. Financial commitment of school and community

6. A mechanism to sustain growth and development of the core group
7. Community leader who serves as "harbor pilot"
8. Empowerment of the core group and appreciation and acceptance of each member's uniqueness

We cannot expect community interventions to be successful when we fail to understand that minimum conditions must exist. In their absence, predictable problems always occur.

Implementing community interventions is difficult, if that is not already obvious. Even when all the obstacles appear to be clearly defined and when predictable problems are thoughtfully mediated, the key to a successful intervention is collaboration. Collaboration is not easy, either. In fact, a most challenging task in the whole scenario of collaboration is just to convene a meeting of people essential to a core group.

To get a better idea of the complexity of convening a meeting, consider what it takes to coordinate a dinner out with four of your favorite couples. For discussion's sake, these four couples all have young children who require baby-sitters. If you have ever tried this, you know that the mere task of arranging a mutually available date for dinner, never mind where all of these different people want to go, is a challenge. Does this sound like work to you? It might be easier to go out alone or stay home!

Most people would rather do something alone, or do nothing at all, than try to coordinate not just one but many meetings; nevertheless, there must be a collective force driven by understanding of and commitment to the concept of primary prevention. But who has time for primary prevention when it is necessary to deal with a tidal wave of human problems and service demands?

14

When Everything
Goes Wrong

Two factors lead me to present one last terrific "sinking." First, there is everything within us that helps us misevaluate whether the minimum conditions exist to successfully implement a primary prevention community intervention. This may be because human service professionals tend to believe the best about people and assume others can work together for the good of the "client." Second, if you are like me, you may need the "club-over-the-head-light-bulb-goes-on" approach to insight.

A Sinking

For several years, I had been in contact with a prevention professional who worked for a regional substance-abuse center in a large urban area. Bob May was responsible for the dissemination of substance abuse–related prevention materials and programs throughout a region that included one large city. During this time, Bob had discussed bringing ROPE into the city.

Bob grew up professionally in his position and was very enthusiastic about and committed to the concept of prevention. During his early years in the job, he had learned important technical and theoretical lessons about primary prevention. Early in Bob's tenure, his enthusiasm and commitment had outdistanced his capacity to understand and deliver effective primary prevention services.

Bob was to become the harbor pilot for bringing the Rite of Passage Experience into a large urban port. It was not apparent initially, but Bob not only had limited familiarity with the harbor, he also barely knew how to navigate. Nevertheless, I sat in the passenger seat, watching the sights as we entered the harbor, absolutely oblivious to the impending disaster.

Bob had organized a community orientation to ROPE. He had identified a particular neighborhood in the city for project implementation and had secured the cooperation and support of the neighborhood center's director, Marie Johnson. I had no idea what to expect as I drove through a housing project and pulled into the parking lot of the neighborhood center. The graffiti-covered walls of the building stood out less than the bars on the windows. There was no name or other identifying mark to distinguish this building from a jail; there was only "Bloods Kill Crips" and "Alphonse Reigns" scrawled over the steel doors.

I was greeted by the loud echoes of children playing, and by a strong smell of disinfectant. I stood in the cavernous hallway and looked around, trying to get my bearings.

"Excuse me. Do you know where there is a meeting?" I asked a man in a blue maintenance uniform.

"Upstairs and to the right. Second door on the left," he said.

I followed his directions and entered a room full of people. I stood at the doorway for a moment, still unsure of my whereabouts.

"Hi, David!"

I heard Bob's voice and then saw his white, smiling face and waving hand emerge from a sea of ethnic faces. Bob came across the room, followed closely by an African American woman. In contrast to Bob, who was rather short, Marie Johnson was tall and powerful-looking. She quickly shook my hand and smiled broadly as we were introduced.

"I'm so glad to finally meet you. Bob's told me so much about ROPE. We're really looking forward to doing it here," she said with friendly authority.

I was immediately impressed by her. As she glided through the room, introducing me, I was relieved to learn that she would be sharing the harbor pilot duties with Bob.

Marie turned and introduced me to a tall, uniformed police officer as she made her way through the throng of people. "This is Rick Johnson, chief of the narcotics division."

Teachers, parents, community organizers, recreation staff, and community-based agency staff stood talking with one another as they ate and drank from a buffet of fruit, chips, dip, and punch. A very nice spread, I thought, as I set up the slide projector and other materials for the presentation.

The presentation seemed to go well. There were several questions, and a brief discussion ensued about the upcoming training and implementation, to be coordinated by Bob and Marie. I was somewhat curious although not very concerned about who would be selected for the training and how. As things turned out, I should have been more curious and concerned.

Several weeks later, Bob told me that Larry, whom he had hired to coordinate the project, would be coordinating training and implementation as well. Bob assured me that Larry was very able to do this and had worked in the community for many years. A few days later, Larry himself called me. He wanted to arrange a meeting to discuss ROPE and the upcoming training. Although he had not been at the community orientation, he said he was very knowledgeable about the community and had grown up in the neighborhood.

About a month later, an associate and I arrived at about half past eight in the morning for the scheduled nine o'clock training. We were supposed to be met by Bob or Larry, to set up the room. Ten minutes later, strolling nervously around the halls of the conference center, I bumped into someone carrying an easel and a large pad of newsprint.

"Are you here for the ROPE training?" I asked somewhat anxiously.

"Yes. I'm Sheila. I work with Bob and Larry," she offered, panting under the weight of her load. "Are you David?"

"Yes. Do you know where we are meeting?"

She mentioned a part of the building where I had already been.

"You mean Larry isn't here yet?" Sheila said. She rolled her eyes and shook her head.

The three of us arrived together at the room, which was locked. Sheila went to find a custodian while my associate and I stood in anxious silence.

"Well, I guess we're off to a blazing start," I said. We both laughed nervously.

"I don't know who made the reservation," I heard Sheila say as she turned the corner with a security guard in tow.

"I'm not really supposed to open the door unless you are on my list," the guard told us.

"Hey! Leroy, my man, what's happening?" Larry's booming voice rang out as he approached.

"Larry. Hey, what are you doing here? Are you with these folks?" the guard asked.

"Yeah. We have a training in here. I called to reserve the room."

"Well, okay, if you say so," the guard said as he quickly unlocked the door.

It was ten minutes to nine as we scrambled to make the necessary adjustments. Curriculum manuals, workbooks, easels, video equipment, nametags, and related training paraphernalia were organized around the room.

"Hi, everybody. Breakfast is here," Bob said jovially, entering the room with a big bag from the local doughnut factory. "Boy, you wouldn't believe the line in that place! Have you ever been there, Sheila?" Bob said, looking hurried and as if he needed a quick connection with someone who might have arrived on time.

"Yeah," Sheila said coolly.

"Who else is here?" Bob asked, searching the room as if expecting to see people under the desks.

"This is it," Larry said. He shrugged. "I don't know where everybody is. I spoke to them just the other day, to remind them."

Larry continued setting up the video equipment, apparently ignoring the fact that it was nine o'clock and no one else was here yet. The thought that no one else might show up had never occurred to me, but that thought now entered my mind, painfully.

"How many people are you expecting, Bob?" I asked, more to ease my discomfort than because I really wanted to know.

"Well, let's see. Larry"— Bob turned to Larry, looking for

support—"we asked the people from the neighborhood community center. You gave the participant questionnaires to Marie? At the community center?"

"Yeah, I spoke to Marie. She said Charles and Reilly were going to participate."

"Okay. So Charles and Reilly are supposed to come, and I think Marie said she'd be here, too," Bob said.

It was now ten past nine. Discomfort began to spread.

"As you can see, we've had a little trouble getting people to participate," Bob finally acknowledged.

"I don't know what's wrong with these people. Jeez!" Larry shrugged his broad shoulders and slumped into his chair. "I contacted all the agencies you told me to, Bob."

My associate and I exchanged glances. I sat quietly, waiting for something to happen that could give me an idea of what to do. A group-process training with only three people was more than even we could manage.

Bob and Larry began to explain that there was some animosity on the part of other community agencies: they resented Bob's agency for getting this and other grants, and they claimed that Larry was not acting professionally in his capacity of project coordinator. By half past nine, we felt that the ship was beginning to sink. Actually, however, it had sunk a long time ago, but we had never stopped to ask the right questions. Finger-pointing and blaming others occupied Larry and Bob while my associate and I stepped outside to regroup.

When we returned, there were two new participants from the neighborhood center, Charles and Reilly. They had joined the group. We pushed forward, dreading the prospect of what the next five days had in store. Five days on a sinking ship could be our worst nightmare.

When we finished our introductions and resumed our dialogue about everyone's expectations for the training, Charles and Reilly both claimed to have no idea of why they were there or what the training was about.

"I was told by Marie to be here. So here I am," Charles said.

"Me, too," Reilly offered.

Larry rolled his eyes and slumped back in his chair.

Over the next hour, we provided another orientation to the concept of primary preventive community intervention. The only excitement came when one other participant arrived at ten o'clock, and we announced a break half an hour later. It felt as if we had been there for days.

Things got no better. The training limped along during the first three days. Participants floated in and out, claiming any number of unforeseen emergencies. Bob did not even stay for the entire training. He claimed an impending grant deadline and wandered in and out over the next five days.

While Bob was gone, Larry began to describe, in more detail, the history of the community agency's struggles. He described Bob's battles with several of the community agency administrators and the difficulty Bob was having because he was white and they were black. Larry painted a picture that graphically illustrated predictable problems. He spoke about mistrust and misunderstanding in the relationships among the community agencies invited to participate in the training. He described several agencies' internal conflicts, which limited communication between agency administrators and direct service workers. This was especially true with respect to the Rite of Passage Experience and created confusion over why staff were being trained.

I did not perceive Larry's remarks as derogatory of Bob or of Bob's agency. Larry tried to present a reason for why people were not showing up and committing themselves to the training. Charles and Reilly confirmed what Larry was describing. In fact, for the first time during the training, they became animated and energetic.

To make the whole sinking worse, the ship later caught fire. Sheila went back to Bob and claimed that Larry was making derogatory and negative remarks about him behind his back. Larry was called into Bob's office, in the middle of the training, and reprimanded. Whatever spark of essential enthusiasm had existed was quickly extinguished. These people were sailing in the opposite direction from the one necessary to fostering the elements essential to a core group.

But, to return to the sinking ship, the last day of training (and I use the word *training* loosely) ensured our doom. I could only imagine that Bob was both trying to be helpful and attempting to regain his control and professional esteem when he invited fifteen new people on the last day.

"I really think this is a great program and want to get more people involved, so they will understand what we are doing," he offered in explanation.

In my best professional style, and avoiding any display of shock or anger, I said, "Oh."

The last two days of the training are designed to give participants an opportunity to practice delivery of the project in the safety of the core group. To the dismay and chagrin of the participants, however, the room began to fill with new people. I instructed those who would be practicing delivery of the project to prepare with their cofacilitators in another room while I tried to figure out what was going on. I introduced myself and asked the new people (about twenty youth workers and teachers) what their expectations were for the day, and how much they knew about the Rite of Passage Experience. What I heard in response was unsettling, to say the least.

The new people said that they had been "summoned" to be there by their respective supervisors, to "review" or "evaluate" or "observe" this new program. They were all uncertain about why they were there. Having had some practice at dancing to this tune during the previous several days, I began to present an overview of primary preventive community intervention and rites of passage. Someone interrupted me after five minutes.

"What kind of certificate are we going to get after today?"

"Excuse me?"

"Are we going to get a certificate or continuing education credits for today?"

"I'm not sure what you mean," I responded, knowing full well what was meant but having no idea what to say.

The room erupted.

"What are we supposed to get out of this?" someone shouted.

"I think you'd better run out and print some certificates," another voice rang out. There was a burst of laughter.

I shifted nervously, trying desperately to figure out how to make the best of the situation. I glanced at Bob, searching for help, for a copilot to help me navigate through the storm. He sat very

still, off to one side of the room. He averted his eyes. He blended
into the wall very nicely. Finally, the solution came to me.

"Let's take a break," I said.

What had happened? To begin with, there was no harbor
pilot. There was never another person in the community who
shared Bob's enthusiasm and desire to see the project successfully
replicated, and this important deficiency set a course straight for the
rocks. Bob and Marie were administrators. They could have provided some leadership and forged connections, but they did not join
to provide a nurturing environment.

There was no respected and acknowledged educational or
community leader who could foster collaboration with and commitment to the successful replication of the project. It is clear that every
one of the ten essential elements was absent. In fact, the project
replication failed so miserably because there was never any consideration of those elements.

Even when most of the essential elements are initially absent,
however, a functional core group can still overcome those deficien-
cies. In fact, it can even create the missing elements after training.
Nevertheless, the disaster that ensued during the establishment of
this core group prevented any chance to create the essential elements, and no amount of time, endurance, or patience could overcome the obstacles. The minimum conditions were never present,
and we had no luck at all.

A number of important questions arise. Can training in and
of itself ever create a core group, or must some intangible element
exist first? Can a functioning core group always create the minimum conditions necessary to implement and sustain a primary
prevention community intervention? Can we ever know all the predictable problems that may confront a community intervention?
These questions, like many in the human services, have no defin-
itive answers; the dynamic ebb and flow of critical variables in a
community system presents many challenges.

Successful implementation of a primary prevention community intervention needs participation and collaboration from peo-

ple, agencies, and systems that may have a long history of conflict, mistrust, and disconnection. It may be difficult to sustain an effort, especially given the tendency for systems to react continually to situations, rather than charting and sticking with reasonable courses of action. Training, no matter how intensive, cannot always produce a core group, especially when community leaders are absent or are not committed to creating and participating in the process in which power is shared.

While much depends on sheer luck, good or bad, there do seem to be predictable problems inherent in planning, implementing, and sustaining a primary prevention community intervention. One of the greatest is the constant demand for human service systems' limited resources, a demand that affects people's time and ability to plan and carry out comprehensive strategies. In the face of this overwhelming demand, commitment to primary prevention always seems to take a back seat. Another problem is that many community systems and agencies have deep, long-standing conflicts, resulting in part from competition for limited funds and fueled by a collective inability to collaborate. Finally, when people and systems do seek to establish preventive interventions, they focus more on concrete programs than on ongoing processes of mutual creation, implementation, and adaptation. They "send out for" and "bring in" packaged programs, slogans, and other limited, "quick fix" approaches, which do more to ease the need to do something quickly than to solve problems. People would rather throw money at a problem and stand behind politically expedient messages than roll up their sleeves for the long haul of implementing a comprehensive primary prevention community intervention.

One significant variable seems to be relationships among community leaders. An idea for an effective primary prevention strategy, whether born inside or outside a system, needs the support and guidance of at least two harbor pilots. Although they are not completely responsible for the creation and maintenance of collaboration, community leaders significantly contribute to a system's ability to collaborate, and their absence invites predictable problems. Turf and power issues, misunderstandings and lack of commitment to primary prevention all lie in the path of a new project.

Parental noninvolvement and political events also affect the new project. All these obstacles can doom the new strategy.

Primary prevention is difficult in and of itself. It occurs in the context of a full range of human service delivery. Given the ongoing, ever-present demands placed on human service providers, is it any wonder that the creative use of comprehensive interventions like ROPE is limited, at best? Who has the time or energy to go the extra distance that primary prevention requires?

The selections of the primary prevention strategy, the Rite of Passage Experience, and the cases were based on their ability to illustrate and convey components essential for the success of a primary prevention community intervention. Although not a pretty sight, the "voyages" that were the most turbulent provide the best examples of predictable problems that surface in the implementation of community interventions.

Primary prevention in the context of human services is not clean and easy. It takes considerable effort, commitment, and collaboration on the part of an entire community to make a positive difference in the lives of its children.

PART IV

Practical Lessons and Future Directions

15

Evaluating the
Rite of Passage Experience

I frequently describe ROPE as a successful or exemplary program, and I recognize that the reader may see these descriptions as biased and devoid of objectivity. Although I have significant biases toward primary prevention in general, and toward the Rite of Passage Experience specifically, my comments are based on a variety of evaluation measures collected over a number of years and reflect ROPE's selection by the National League of Cities (1987) and the State of Connecticut Office of Policy and Management (1987) as an exemplary program. It has recently (1992) been selected by the Child Welfare League of America for inclusion in their program exchange.

I will not attempt here to discuss the challenge to research in the area of primary prevention, although I will say that it is significant. I also will not engage in a lengthy discussion of the merits or limitations of the research reported here. I wish only to note that the Rite of Passage Experience has been the subject of research that reflects its promise as a viable intervention.

Quantitative and qualitative research data have been collected and analyzed on the Rite of Passage Experience since 1982. Included here are reports on several studies. I have occasionally offered brief explanations, to make the data and analysis easier to read. Only those quantitative results that achieved statistical significance are highlighted.

Unfortunately, there have been no efforts to investigate the impact of training and the intervention on the development of a working core group. If we consider the importance of developing core groups in a community, then such examination would seem extremely valuable. Countless descriptive reports from parents, teachers, counselors, and students offer further evidence of the intervention's positive impact. Studies currently under way investigate the impact of ROPE on the outcome of psychotherapy with students and their families. Early indications are promising in this area as well.

Quantitative Study

One study consisting of a series of reports was conducted through a grant from the State of Connecticut Office of Policy and Management. In this study, 5 cohorts of ROPE students, including a total of 410 subjects, were reported on between 1986–1989. Each experimental cohort contained 52 students (1986), 75 students (1987), 56 students (1988), and 54 students (1989). The 1986 report describes the research methodology as follows: "In this study a pretest/posttest repeated measures research design was employed. Thus, the same measures were administered before the start of the program (to assess baseline scores of the subjects prior to the intervention), and after the intervention was completed. The entire 6th grade population from an elementary school served as the experimental group. Another school's 6th grade was selected on the basis of demographic similarity and was employed as the control group" (Hawkins, 1986, p. 1).
      Before the measures were planned,

> the researcher conducted a review of the literature to locate existing questionnaires that would measure the relevant attitudes and traits. No appropriate measures were found to assess the desired constructs in the relevant age group. Thus, four questionnaires were constructed for the study. The attitudes and traits measured include: 1) alienation and anomie vs. connectedness and belonging via a 50-item scale titled "How I Feel About the World"; 2) and 3) self-esteem and self-efficacy

vs. inferiority and incompetence via a 45-item scale titled "What I'm Like" and a 13-item scale titled "How I Describe Myself"; and 4) prosocial values vs. antisocial values via a 19-item scale titled "How I Believe I Should Behave." These scales were developed by gathering from the literature a variety of measures used to assess similar or related constructs and selecting from these instruments items that were most relevant to the current study. In addition to these measures, two sets of scales from the University of Washington Youth Survey were used. Four scales, measuring involvement with family and attachment to family, school, and peers were combined in the section titled "How I Feel About Other People." Three scales, measuring delinquent behavior, misbehavior, and alcohol and marijuana use, were combined in the section titled "Some Things I've Done."

Testing sessions were administered by the evaluation consultant on a classroom by classroom basis. Each session took about 45 minutes. Data were scored, entered into the computer, and analyzed for group differences (via descriptive statistics such as means, frequencies, and correlations, and via hypothesis testing statistics such as repeated measures analysis of variance) [Hawkins, 1986, p. 12].

Each year a preliminary report of findings was prepared on the basis of the analysis of each cohort. Some preliminary reports identified statistically significant results in some areas, but not in others. Each preliminary study included approximately fifty to sixty students in a control group and an experimental group. Some of the results included in the preliminary reports of findings were as follows:

Involvement with Family, 1986

The analysis of this scale showed a statistically significant effect of group by time (F (1,68) 5.01, $p < .03$). Examination of the means showed that the ROPE group increased their ratings of family involvement by 4% while the control group decreased their ratings by 7%. Thus, participants in the program reported being more involved and better able to communicate with their parents after the program, while the control group reported becoming less involved and less able to communicate with their parents by the end of the school year [p. 3].

Attachment to School, 1986

The analysis of this scale showed a significant change over time (F (1,68) 15.95, $p < .0002$), and a significant group-by-time interaction (F (1,68) 11.04, $p < .001$). Examination of the means showed that, while attachment to school went down over time for the sample as a whole, the drop in ratings was only 2% for the ROPE group (which is insignificant), but was 33% for the control group. Thus, students in the ROPE program reported more positive school attitudes following the program than the control group reported [p. 4].

Drug and Alcohol Use, 1986

Analysis of this variable showed a significant effect of time (F (1,68) 5.33, $p < .02$), with substance use increasing over time. However, inspection of the means shows the following trends. The ROPE girls increased their substance use by 78%, from an average of 1.04 to 1.85% times per month, while the control girls increased by 176%, from an average of 1.42 to 3.92 times per month. The ROPE boys increased their substance use by 3.9% from 2.55 to 2.65 times per month, while the control boys increased by 86.5%, from 1.92 to 3.58 times per month [p. 6].

Knowledge Test, 1986

There was a significant effect of group on the summary score formed from the individual knowledge items (F (1,67) 19.53, $p < .0001$). The ROPE group had an average score of 15.38 on the knowledge test, while the control group had an average score of 7.14. There was also marginally significant group-by-sex effect (R (1,67) 2.79, $p < .10$), indicating the ROPE girls (average score 17.15) did better on the knowledge test compared to ROPE boys (average score 14.17), while control girls did somewhat worse (average score 6.27) compared to control boys (average score 8.10). ROPE subjects also rated their liking of the program, whether they thought the program should be offered to all 6th grade students, and whether they thought the program should be continued in 7th grade. On a 1-to-6 scale (with 1 indicating the student "didn't like the program at all" and 6 indicating the student "really liked the program a lot"), the average score across all participants was 5.38. The average opinion about whether the program should be continued in 7th grade was 3.69, somewhere between a 3, "it probably should" and a 4, "it definitely should." Similarly, the participants thought all the 6th-grade students should have the ROPE program (mean score 3.64, with 3 = "it probably should," and 4 = "it definitely should") [p. 8].

Drug and Alcohol Use, 1987

There was a marginally significant effect of program versus control status on this measure (F (1,67) 2.72, $p < .10$). Inspection of the means shows that the ROPE students decreased their rate of drug use by 60%, while control students increased theirs by 57% [Hawkins, 1987, p. 6].

Major Delinquency, 1988

There was a significant effect of the program for this scale, (F (1,80) 9.52, $p < .003$). Inspection of the means showed that the number of delinquent acts increased among the ROPE students from .47 at time one to .55 at time two (which is actually no increase at all), while they increased from .47 to 4.27 among the control students [Hawkins, 1988, p. 4].

Minor Delinquency/Misbehavior Scale, 1988

There was a significant effect of group over time on the number of acts reported, (F (1,80) 4.04, $p < .048$). Examination of the means shows that for the ROPE students, acts of misbehavior increased from 2.4 at time 1 to 4.4 at time 2, while for the control students, acts of misbehavior showed a greater proportional increase, from 7 to 18 [p. 4].

Drug and Alcohol Use, 1988

Analysis of this variable showed a significant effect of group over time (F (1,80) 9.24, $p < .003$). Inspection of the means shows that alcohol and drug consumption increased for the ROPE group from an average of 1.27 to 1.57 times per month, while the control group increased at a much higher rate, from an average of 2.38 to 9.96 times per month [p. 4].

Attachment to School, 1989

There was a significant effect of the program (R (1,82) 3.34, $p < .07$). Examination of the means shows that while both groups' scores declined over time, for the ROPE students, rating dropped by only 6.4%, while scores for the control group students dropped by 15.5%, indicating that ROPE participants became less alienated from school than control students [Hawkins, 1989a, p. 2].

Anomie and Alienation Versus Connectedness and Belonging, 1989

This scale showed a significant effect of program (F (1,82) 6.73, $p < .01$), with program students reporting a heightened sense of connectedness and belonging after the program, whereas the control students reported more alienation over time [1989a, p. 3].

Combining the Data from All Cohorts, 1986–1989

The program showed a pattern of results similar to those of the individual years: significant results in one or two scales, trends in some others, and no differences between the groups in the remainder. The Drug and Alcohol scale showed highly significant differences, as it did in Cohort 3 data. There were trends in the following scales: Involvement with Family, Attachment to Family, Attachment to School, Delinquency, and

Values. Attachment to Peers, Misbehavior, Alienation, and Self-Concept showed no result [Hawkins, 1989b, p. 3].

Qualitative Reports

Which variables are critical to behavioral and attitudinal change? What measurement instrument can assess the impact of the strategy on the most salient variables? The need for further quantitative research is obvious. There are, however, significant qualitative data (that is, descriptive responses of parents, teachers, and students), which strongly point to a positive impact for the Rite of Passage Experience.

What follows is a glimpse of parents', teachers', and students' responses to questions about ROPE (Blumenkrantz, 1988). The questions were designed to assess students' enjoyment of the program, their learning from the program, and their opinions about whether the program should be continued. The brief excerpts that follow are consistent with responses from thousands of other students who have participated in the program during the past decade, their parents, and their teachers. During collection of posttest quantitative data, participants in the same experimental group, their parents, and their teachers were asked a series of questions.

In response to the question "Rate your overall enjoyment of the ROPE sessions (1 = lowest, 5 = highest)," 88 percent of 153 students reported receiving high or highest enjoyment from ROPE (p. 3). This is consistent with another report, where 88.9 percent of 134 students reported receiving high or highest enjoyment from ROPE (Reslock, 1989, p. 3).

Students were asked, "Describe clearly at least two things you learned or felt as a result of the program." About 50 percent of 153 students responded that they had learned about cooperation, working well with a group, self-confidence or belief in power to do things once thought difficult or impossible, making decisions, and trust (Blumenkrantz, 1988). Students reported over seventy different discoveries during ROPE. Some of their other responses were "to have confidence in yourself and other people," "treat others as you would want to be treated," "I can make a decision on what to do and not worry about peer pressure," "I learned to work in a group

160 — Fulfilling the Promise of Children's Services

and even with people I don't like," "If you listen to others' ideas, you can come up with better answers," and "I learned that I am useful and can be a big help or problem."

Parents' responses also indicated strong support and belief in the value of ROPE for their children. Over 93 percent of parents reported that their children had enjoyed the program very much. Over 85 percent of parents reported that the ROPE program had been of great value to their children.

In the same study, parents reported that ROPE "increased my child's self-confidence, aided his/her personal insights, has helped or will help my child cope with the problems of adolescence and will ease the transition from sixth grade to the middle school" (pp. 8, 16, 23).

Other comments included the following: "I think ROPE is a *fantastic* program. There should be more programs like this in the school system. It's a real-life learning situation." "My son brought home his experiences and new knowledge every night after he had a ROPE class. And it was discussed for days after." "I think ROPE is an excellent program and would like to see it continued. With this type of program the kids are learning while having fun. This is the first year my daughter insists on going to school even when she's ill."

Teachers' responses, reported in the same study, were consistent with parents' and students' results: "Student learning included: teaches children how to solve a problem, get along, make decisions, trust, plan, cooperate and work together." The report goes on to say, "Several comments revolved around teacher, principal and community agency relationships, which were seen to benefit" (p. 3).

In another study, teachers reported the following benefits of the program: "brainstorming problem solving techniques carry over into the classroom; helped build self-esteem; children working cooperatively towards one goal; children achieve personal goals; students looked forward to discussing their concerns with someone who would listen, understand and guide them" (Reslock, 1989, p. 1).

Measurement

Appropriate measurement techniques remain a challenge. Instruments have to assess change in parents, teachers, students, and a community. The complexity of a comprehensive strategy may present insurmountable challenges to research. How would one quantitatively measure art? What is the value of a student's comment that "ROPE is the best thing to come along since comic books"?

Again, the Rite of Passage Experience is not a panacea. The quantitative and qualitative results reported here are intended to illustrate some of the benefits of the intervention, captured by the measurement instruments employed.

16

♔

People Helping People

A considerable amount of time, effort, and money has been expended for innumerable organizations and agencies to conduct independent and isolated searches for answers to social problems. People seek quick-and-easy solutions and search for leaders to deliver them. Political leaders and education and other human service agencies have failed to effectively collaborate in order to significantly help children and families. If there are solutions, and this is a tentative proposition, they are discoverable in the process of the collaborative search— that is, people working together to help people.

It is a cold, hard fact that, despite all our knowledge about children, families, communities, schools, and primary prevention, we have not appreciably improved the lot of children in this country during the past several decades. In fact, it can be argued that the children of today may be less advantaged than those of yesteryear. In larger and larger numbers, children are entering school woefully unprepared socially and emotionally. The first babies born to cocaine-addicted parents have entered our schools. In single-parent families, and in two-parent working families, babies who will live the first five years of their lives without benefit of a national child and family policy are becoming the majority. Children are entering the educational system without a secure psychological foundation to support their continued positive development. Kindergarten and first-grade teachers all across the country know what I am talking about. They live it daily in their classrooms as they try to attend to more and more difficult and disturbed children.

Families have changed, too, and are not effectively transmitting the attitudes and beliefs useful in promoting children's successful entry into the adult world. Moreover, schools, churches, businesses, and organized activities for youth are often inadequate. But these statements all miss the point.

The point, in the simplest terms, is that people in human services agencies and systems must forgo the desire for *personal* independence, control, power, and rewards. They must work *together* to create the necessary supports and opportunities for communities and families to help children successfully cross the threshold from childhood to adulthood.

Human services, at the most elementary level, are about one person helping another. More often than not, however, systems, agencies, and human service policy development are shaped by the personalities of leaders who hold the reins of power. Personality clashes and difficulty collaborating will significantly affect the delivery of human services.

Everyone Is an Expert

Leadership is difficult enough, but now everyone seems to be an expert in human services. Everyone has something to say, especially when it comes to the question What's the matter with kids today? (In these instances, an ounce of pretense is worth more than a pound of manure.) People tend to discuss human service issues (education, psychology, welfare, social security, and the like) with a level of passion not typically found in discussions of other technical or professional topics. Let the conversation turn to the problem of kids today, the elderly, social security, or welfare, and everyone knows why the problems exist and how to solve them.

The tool of the trade in human services is language. Most of us have at least minimal language abilities, and when a psychological principle or piece of technical knowledge is described well, most people will respond, "I know that. What's the big deal?" Our human ability to communicate makes psychological principles understandable to a large number of people, as part of being human.

Most human service agencies, educational systems, and human service systems are governed by boards, commissions, or committees that have policymaking authority. Members of these governing bodies usually have little formal training in the particular human service areas, however. They tend to rely on personal experience, and their life experiences serve as points of reference, enabling them to impart "expert" guidance in setting policy. But think of what would happen if the delivery of surgical services were actively governed by a policymaking body of laypersons with no medical training. Imagine what would happen if the members of this governing body were elected and wholeheartedly believed that they understood the field of medicine and the practice of surgery. Would you trust your body to this kind of surgical service?

Collaboration becomes a critical focus at the policy level. How well people collaborate in understanding the problems of living, and how well they use their understanding in the development of workable responses, may determine the effectiveness of the entire human service enterprise.

How can we institutionalize collaboration in a society that prizes individualism? There is a widespread and mistaken assumption that people will automatically collaborate for the benefit of others, especially children. Collaboration is not automatic, however, even if people are assigned, appointed, or directed to work together. Minimum conditions for collaboration must exist or be promoted (see Chapter Ten). It is no accident that this book focuses so much on the presence of a core group, its composition, and its function. Regardless of the programmatic strength of a primary prevention strategy, the absence of a core group will diminish and probably undermine the program's effectiveness. Establishing the core group requires a community's understanding and commitment to collaboration, the first of the ten minimum conditions for the development, implementation, maintenance, and growth of a primary prevention community intervention (see Chapter Nine).

Collaboration cannot be legislated, and a good illustration of this truth is the recent attempt to modify the 1976 legislation that created the Youth Service Bureau. This modification was intended to enhance a community's ability to work collaboratively for the development and provision of a comprehensive range of youth- and family-related services. In 1990, when this slight modification was proposed, legislators were bombarded by complaints from state agencies, police chiefs, schools, and a host of other human service-related constituents. The change provided for a coordinating function in the Youth Service Bureaus. As had been true before (see Chapter Two), key components of the community saw no need (and did not want) to be coordinated. Coordination was interpreted as control, rather than as a mechanism for promoting collaboration—people working together for the good of the community and its children.

The notion of community collaboration is not new. For a long time, it has been accepted as essential to the development and delivery of comprehensive human services. In an apparent attempt to promote collaboration, many funders of human service programs call for the establishment of advisory councils or committees, which must be characterized by broad representation of the community. Nevertheless, each new funding requirement seems to spawn yet another new advisory committee. Rarely are these committees connected, and even more rarely does one central committee serve as an advisory group for all such grants. "Paper committees" (they frequently exist only as names on a list) cannot precipitate and sustain collaboration. It is always easier and less effective to sign someone up for a committee after the decision has been made about what the committee will do; it is much more difficult—and certainly more threatening to a leader—to create a committee that has any real decision-making ability and is empowered to ensure that something really happens. In and of itself, the creation of a committee does not guarantee collaboration.

Federal, state, and private funding sources rarely require community coordination and collaboration for the development and implementation of comprehensive human services, especially effective primary prevention. In fact, limited grant money usually requires community agencies to compete. Moreover, the short time frame for grant preparation and submission usually precludes any true development of collaborative relationships. Not uncommonly, a grant proposal must be submitted within four to six weeks after the grant information and application are obtained. Furthermore, in all too many cases, the availability of funding is the driving force behind the implementation of human service initiatives.

Money: The Great Determinant of Program Development

Obviously, money is the life blood of human services, but what happens in an agency when a funded program is no longer needed, has served its purpose, or is determined to be ineffective? It is the rare agency that turns back funding because it has judged one of its programs to be unnecessary or inadequate. Programs may be perpetuated simply to continue funding.

The potential for dependence on funding sources is a critical issue, one that will require a shift in thinking for funding sources and human service agencies alike. Funding plans that provide for strong development and evaluation, coupled with greater movement toward local financial support of primary prevention and other efforts, may deserve investigation. Whether the national and state policy of competitive application processes is a side effect of free enterprise and the capitalist system is unclear. What is clear is that there is nothing to stem the epidemic of independent programs, operated by autonomous, disconnected, noncoordinated systems and agencies, that produce nothing remotely like viable, comprehensive human service delivery. In fact, such slogans as "war on drugs" and "just say no," to name just two, do much to encourage ineffective responses.

An Infrastructure Built on Quicksand

One could conclude that inadequate policy exists at all levels of government for the creation of a viable, effective, and coordinated human service infrastructure, especially one that promotes and sustains prevention. Is it that we do not have the will to marshal our resources and develop comprehensive human service delivery systems? Do we have any idea of what such a system would look like in the first place? I doubt that there is any clear, easy answer to either question.

We may reap some insights if we consider the parallels between the development of a physical infrastructure (roads, bridges, and transportation systems) and a human service infrastructure. The development of both infrastructures requires a policy decision, a decision that says it is good to move people from point A to point B, whether that point is a geographical location or some human condition.

Policymakers do not typically tell a department of transportation or engineers how to build roads or bridges. Once a policy decision is made, a plan is developed, blueprints of the transportation system are designed, and construction begins. Years and sometimes decades pass; the time depends on the complexity and size of the construction project. The original plans usually are not altered, and the project stays on course until its completion.

Things are less concrete in human services. In fact, much debate exists at the policy level about the human condition and how and if people even should be moved from one point to another. When a policy does exist, there are always divergent views on how to enact it. We seem incapable of enacting any plan over a long period to alter the human condition appreciably. We have, however, created immense bureaucracies and disconnected systems, all attempting to move people to some "better" human condition.

The continued compartmentalization of human service delivery, directed at distinct populations (children, adults, elderly people) and across specific symptoms, limits the sharing of resources and fosters competitive, noncooperative relationships among service providers in communities. This compartmentalization is abetted by existing federal policy, which establishes separate agencies to oversee and regulate business in each of the human service areas.

We continue to pay little attention to the human experience itself, which calls for connectedness, not only among people but also among the systems and agencies responsible for providing care and service to other human beings. Isn't it about time we moved beyond the attitude that says there are enough problems to go around? Given the increasing number and severity of problems facing our children, it should be clear that the only viable responses will come from collective community efforts.

One collective community effort, the Rite of Passage Experience, offers a vehicle to help communities transmit essential skills, knowledge, and beliefs to children. A central strategy in human experience—rituals of initiation—has been forgotten, perhaps because of attempts to find "quick fixes" or technologies to help us raise our children. The Rite of Passage Experience illustrates the complexity of a comprehensive primary prevention community intervention. It also demonstrates the characteristic difficulty that communities face in implementing a collaborative strategy, and it highlights the minimum conditions for implementing a primary prevention community intervention.

There are no slick, easy-to-do programs for solving human problems. Cookbook-style, never-fail recipes for facilitating communities' efforts to help families and children do not exist. If the human service field is to make a significant difference in the lives of children and families, there must be collective resolve to collaborate and commit our resources to comprehensive primary prevention strategies. People must learn to dance together in pursuit of workable answers to the problems of living. There are no panaceas. There are just people helping people.

FEIFFER COPYRIGHT 1979 Jules Feiffer. Reprinted with permission of Universal Press Syndicate. All rights reserved.

References

Blumenkrantz, D. G. (1988). *Rite of Passage Experience: East Hartford Youth Service Department three-year review and summary.* Unpublished manuscript, Office of Policy and Management, Hartford, CT.

Executives on the way to the top. (1970, April 27). *Newsweek*, p. 80.

Hale, A. (1988). *National Safety Network international data base.* Bellefontaine, OH: National Safety Network.

Hawkins, J. (1986). *Preliminary report on the evaluation of the ROPE Program, August 29, 1986.* Unpublished manuscript, Yale University, New Haven, CT.

Hawkins, J. (1987). *Preliminary report on the evaluation of the ROPE Program (year 2), December 2, 1987.* Unpublished manuscript, Yale University, New Haven, CT.

Hawkins, J. (1988). *Report on the evaluation of the ROPE Program, Cohort 3, November 29, 1988.* Unpublished manuscript, Yale University, New Haven, CT.

Hawkins, J. (1989a). *Report on the evaluation of the ROPE Program, Cohort 5, September 1, 1989.* Unpublished manuscript, Yale University, New Haven, CT.

Hawkins, J. (1989b). *Report on the evaluation of the ROPE Program combined data, Cohorts 1 through 5, October 1, 1989.* Unpublished manuscript, Yale University, New Haven, CT.

Hawkins, J. D., Haggerty, K. P., & Catalano, R. F. (in press). Mobilizing communities to reduce risks for drug abuse: Lessons on using research to guide prevention practice. *Journal of Primary Prevention.*

Norman, S. (1972). *The youth service bureau.* Washington, DC: National Council on Crime and Delinquency.

Price, R. H., Cowen, E. L., Lorion, R. P., & Ramos-McKay, J. (Eds.). (1988). *Fourteen ounces of prevention.* Washington, DC: American Psychological Association.

Reslock, B. (1989). *Three-school winter/spring ROPE evaluation.* Unpublished manuscript, Wethersfield Department of Youth Service, Wethersfield, CT.

Shilts, R. (1987). *And the band played on: Politics, people, and the AIDS epidemic.* New York: St. Martin's Press.

Willis, R. (1985, December). Peak experience: Managers in the mountains. *Management Review*, pp. 18–23.

Selected Readings

Anderson, S. A., & Bagarozzi, D. A. (1989). *Family myths: Psychotherapeutic implications.* New York: Haworth.

Bagarozzi, D. A., & Anderson, S. A. (1989). *Personal, marital, and family myths: Theoretical formulations and clinical strategies.* New York: Norton.

Bates, V. (1987). East Hartford ROPE. In V. Bates (Ed.), *Bringing out the best in kids* (p. 67). Hartford, CT: Office of Policy and Management, State of Connecticut.

Bennis, W., & Nanus, B. (1985). *Leaders.* New York: HarperCollins.

Blumenkrantz, D., & Reslock, B. (1981). *Rite of Passage Experience (ROPE).* Glastonbury, CT: Associates in Counseling & Training.

Campbell, J., & Moyers, B. D. (1988). *The power of myth.* New York: Doubleday.

Demos, J. (1986). *Past, present, and personal: The family and the life course in American history.* New York: Oxford University Press.

Edelwich, J., & Brodsky, A. (1980). *Burnout: Stages of disillusionment in the helping professions.* New York: Human Science Press.

Ehlers, A. P. (1976). *Administration for the human services.* New York: HarperCollins.

Eliade, M. (1958). *Rites and symbols of initiation* (W. R. Trask, Trans.). New York: HarperCollins.

173

Erikson, E. H. (1950). *Childhood and society.* New York: Norton.

Erikson, E. H. (1968). *Identity: Youth and crisis.* New York: Norton.

Felner, R. D., Jason, L. A., Moritsugu, J. N., & Farber, S. S. (1983). Preventive psychology: Evolution and current status. In R. D. Felner, L. A. Jason, J. N. Moritsugu, & S. S. Farber (Eds.), *Preventive psychology: Theory, research, and action* (pp. 3–10). Elmsford, NY: Pergamon Press.

Felner, R. D., Primavera, J., & Cauce, A. M. (1983). The impact of school transitions: A focus for preventive efforts. *American Journal of Community Psychology, 9,* 449–459.

Garner, L. H., Jr. (1989). *Leadership in human services: How to articulate and implement a vision to achieve results.* San Francisco: Jossey-Bass.

Glenn, H. S., & Nelsen, J. (1987). *Raising children for success: Blueprints and building blocks for developing capable people.* Fair Oaks, CA: Sunrise Press.

Jessor, R., Collins, M. I., & Jessor, S. L. (1972). On becoming a drinker: Social-psychological aspects of an adolescent transition. *Annual of the New York Academy of Sciences, 197,* 199–213.

Kett, J. F. (1977). *Rites of passage: Adolescence in America, 1790 to the present.* New York: Basic Books.

Kyle, J. (1987). The Rite of Passage Experience. In J. Kyle (Ed.), *Children, families, and cities: Programs that work at the local level* (pp. 181–183). Washington, DC: National League of Cities.

Levine, M., & Levine, A. (1970). *A social history of helping services: Clinic, school and community.* East Norwalk, CT: Appleton and Lange.

Lewis, C. E., & Lewis, M. A. (1984). Peer pressure and risk-taking behaviors in children. *American Journal of Public Health, 74,* 580–584.

Lofquist, W. (1983). *Discover the meaning of prevention: A practical approach to positive change.* Tucson, AZ: Associates in Youth Development.

Mahdi, L. C., Foster, S., & Little, M. (1987). *Betwixt & between: Patterns of masculine and feminine initiation.* La Salle, IL: Open Court.

Postman, N. (1982). *The disappearance of childhood.* New York: Delacorte Press.

Quinn, W. H., Newfield, N. A., & Protinsky, H. O. (1985). Rites of passage in families with adolescents. *Family Process, 24*, 101–111.

Rainman-Schindler, E., & Lippitt, R. (1980). *Building the collaborative community: Mobilizing citizens for action.* Riverside: University of California Extension.

Roberts, W. O. (1982). *Initiation to adulthood: An ancient rite of passage in contemporary form.* New York: Pilgrim.

Sarason, S. B. (1972). *The creation of settings and the future of societies.* San Francisco: Jossey-Bass.

Sarason, S. B. (1974). *The psychological sense of community: Prospects for a community psychology.* San Francisco: Jossey-Bass.

Sarason, S. B., Carroll, C. F., Maton, K., Cohen, S., & Lorentz, E. (1977). *Human services and resource networks: Rationale, possibilities, and public policy.* San Francisco: Jossey-Bass.

Seltzer, W. J. (1988). Myths of destruction: A cultural approach to families in therapy. *Journal of Psychotherapy and the Family, 4*, 17–34.

U.S. Department of Health, Education and Welfare. (1973). *A review of two hundred youth service bureaus.* Washington, DC: U.S. Department of Health, Education and Welfare.

Van Gennep, A. (1960). *The rites of passage.* Chicago: University of Chicago Press.

Watzlawick, P., Beavin, J. H., & Jackson, D. D. (1967). *Pragmatics of human communication: A study of interactional patterns, pathologies, and paradoxes.* New York: Norton.

Weissman, H. (1973). *Overcoming mismanagement in the human service professions: A casebook of staff initiatives.* San Francisco: Jossey-Bass.

Index

177